FIELD MANUAL
Iowa Farmer's Guide to Legal Issues

Pat Dillon

"This publication is designed to provide general information prepared by professionals in regard to the subject matter covered. It is sold with the understanding that the publisher is not engaged in rendering legal, accounting or other professional service. Although prepared by professionals, the publication should not be utilized as a substitute for a professional service in specific situations. If legal advice or other expert assistance is required, the service of a professional should be sought."

(From a Declaration of Principles jointly adopted by a Committee of the American Bar Association and a Committee of Publishers)

Original sources of authority should be consulted by attorneys or other professionals dealing with specific legal matters.

NO CLAIM TO U.S. GOVERNMENT WORKS

NO CLAIM TO STATE GOVERNMENT WORKS.

This book is designed for farmers, agribusinesses, and their advisors, but it is not a substitute for individual legal advice. No attorney-client relationship is intended or established by reading this material. Always confer with an attorney and the appropriate state or federal agency, to ascertain the current status of the law. Every effort has been made to include up-to-date information, but the law is not static – it is in a constant state of flux. Research and background materials were completed in December 2011.

Copyright © 2012 Pat Dillon

All rights reserved.

ISBN: 1467957577

ISBN-13: 9781467957571

Library of Congress Control Number: 2011961305

CreateSpace, North Charleston, SC

DEDICATION

To SPD, KSD and KGD.

CONTENTS

Acknowledgments vii

Introduction ix

1 Soils and Drainage 1

2 Animals 7

3 Farm patents, copyrights and trademarks 21

4 Bankruptcy 27

5 Contracts 35

6 Farm transportation issues 43

7 Estate Planning 53

8 Getting Paid 65

9 Commodity Sales 69

10 Grain Indemnity and Dealer Licensing 75

11 Insurance 81

12 Labor and the Law 89

13 Farm Lease Basics 99

14 Multi-Peril Crop Insurance Basics 115

15 Planning 119

16	Real Estate	133
17	Regulation of Agriculture	149
	Bibliography	157
	About the Author	161

ACKNOWLEDGMENTS

I would like to acknowledge my friends and family, who provided insight and guidance in the creation of this book, along with the members of the Mastermind group, who spurred this idea to development.

CREDITS

Editor: Valerie Bock, JD
Indexer: Jenny Halteman, Jigsaw Indexing
Front Cover Photo Jessica Rilling
Rear cover Photo: Shelly Ann Dillon

INTRODUCTION

The World of Ag Law

What is the only segment of the economy with a cabinet-level division of government devoted to it? The answer is Agriculture. From the regulation of food preparation to the use of food aid as a foreign policy tool, agriculture and the laws surrounding it impact all of us, every day, whether we like to admit it or not.

The term agricultural law may not be as common as personal injury law or divorce law, but make no mistake - agriculture and the law are forever intertwined. It naturally follows that wherever there is government action creating legal issues, so there will be lawyers, advocating for their clients.

If you're a farmer in Iowa, you'll encounter legal issues in a wide variety of agriculture-related settings, from fertilizer storage to tax withholding for farm labor, and just about every situation in-between. To prevent problems before they happen, you absolutely have to be aware of the circumstances that could, potentially, create legal issues for you or your farm operation. In other words, you need to know at least a little bit about a whole lot of laws related to agriculture and agricultural production, and you need to be willing to seek help from a dedicated agricultural law specialist, when the situation tells you that it is time to do so.

This resource aims to touch on the basics of various segments of agricultural law, identify the potential impact to an Iowa farmer's operations, and hopefully, provide you with a reference that will help you protect and guide your operation toward greater productivity.

1 SOIL AND DRAINAGE ISSUES

Federal Environmental Protection Laws

Regulations of Soils

If you run afoul of government rules regarding soils, you will not be eligible for farm program payments, so it is best to be very cautious, if you think you may have an issue with any of these laws.

"**Sodbuster**" is the nickname given to a federal provision that requires any **highly erodible land (HEL)** producing a product after 1985 to have a **conservation plan** in place and follow that plan. The conservation plan needs to be approved by the Natural Resources Conservation Service (NRCS), a federal government agency.

Use of Wetlands

If you violate federal wetland regulations, you could lose benefits for all farm programs, unless this penalty is waived by the government. Again, it is extremely important that you keep an eye out for possible legal problems, if your property includes wetlands.

"**Swampbuster**" is the nickname of another federal law, also administered by the NRCS, that does not allow the draining, clearing, or filling of **wetlands**, after December 23, 1985. A wetland ground must have hydric soils, hydrophytic vegetation and wetland hydrology. Any conversion of this kind of land, with or without cropping, is enough to run afoul of this law. However, some kinds of changes that were already made to wetland ground before December 23, 1985, can possibly make that land eligible for your use.

To recognize potential legal problems you could face over wetland usage, it can be helpful to understand the NRCS lingo in this area. Here are a few basic terms you should become very familiar with:

Prior Converted (PC): Because there are *no cropping restrictions on PCs*, it is important to find out whether your land is a PC. A PC is a wetland which, prior to December 23, 1985, was:

- Converted to a non-wetland state;
- Had been used at least once to produce an agricultural commodity; and
- As of that date, did not support woody vegetation.

Artificial Wetlands (AW): AWs are wetland areas created due to the activities of humans. Again, there are *no restrictions on cropping AWs*.

Farmed Wetlands (FW): FWs are wetlands which were cropped, but not completely converted, prior to December 23, 1985. Although FWs still meet the definition of a wetland, *farming activity can continue* on wetlands like these, as long as *no additional drainage* is conducted.

> *Note: With FWs, it can be wise to take good notes and identify what the FW area looks like. If it naturally drains out over time, and you do not document the changes as they happen, then the next, new NRCS agent who arrives is going to be asking a lot of questions about how you plan to prove that you have permission to farm this wetland. Make sure you have the records you need, to support your actions.*

It is the landowner's responsibility to comply with the law, and the best insurance against legal problems is to ask for a *wetland determination* from the NRCS. Some owners who've done this before may have to do it again, because wetland determinations completed prior to July 3, 1996, are not considered "certified," and therefore, may not be valid.

Likewise, you can ask for a *sodbuster determination*. The NRCS will issue a form *AD-1026*, which should be kept safely, because it serves as your proof that you are complying with the law.

Building and Operating on Wetlands

Farm buildings may be placed on a filled wetland if a Section 404 permit is obtained and Permit Number 40 is issued. *Farm operations* may also need a Section 404 permit for *utility line back fill, bank*

stabilization, road work, or creek crossing work, when these activities impact navigable bodies of water. Most normal plowing, seeding and harvesting activities are exempt.

The **Conservation Reserve Program (CRP)** is a program that pays landowners to place **HEL lands** into trees, grasses and cover during the time of enrollment. Some taking of hay is authorized. Mowing is only authorized during set time periods allowed by the NRCS.

CRP contracts that are over five years old can be terminated early, but only if:

- The contract started after 1995;
- The land has an erodiblity index of 14 or less; and
- The land is not a field windbreak, grass waterway, filter strip, shelterbelt or bottom land timber area, enrolled as a wetland, or located within 100 feet of a stream.

There are more NRCS programs, including the Wetland Reserve Program (WEP), Conservation Reserve Enhancement Program (CREP), and the Environmental Quality Incentives Program (EQIP), and others. As funding and rules change, it is best consult the local NRCS office for the up-to-date information about these programs.

Iowa Environmental Protection Laws

Iowa controls soil and water issues through the establishment of ***Soil Conservation Districts***. These districts then establish what practices and rates of soil loss are acceptable. Each one of the 100 districts has a Soil Commission, governed by five elected commissioners from the district. The Soil Commission can conduct surveys, investigations, research and demonstrations. The Commission may also construct, improve, or maintain structures, to conserve soil resources.

Disturbing the Ground

Before you disturb the ground, be mindful of Soil Commission rules, which can require you to submit an affidavit, prior to disturbing soil, to show that your activity will not exceed ***soil loss limits***.

Water Storage

Water storage is regulated by the state of Iowa. If you don't comply with state water regulations, you can be fined, and fines for water issues can be up to $25,000 for each day that the violation continues.

While not a giant concern in most years, water is an essential part of production agriculture, and you may be tempted to house water for a non-rainy year, but note that anyone who **withdraws** over 25,000 gallons a day or **stores** more than 18 acre feet of water needs a **water use permit** from the Department of Natural Resources (DNR). This permit may limit use during times of low flow or draught. **Diverting water** directly into an aquifer also requires a permit. **Wells** require a permit prior to being dug or replaced. **Abandoned wells** should be plugged. **Ag drainage wells** do not need a permit, but need to be registered with the DNR.

Water Quality

Iowa's DNR also regulates **ground water contamination.** Farm operators can avoid claims of ground water contamination claims, but you must be careful to:

- Apply nitrogen only in the amounts indicated by soil tests and label instructions; and
- Apply pesticides according to label and with the correct applicator's license.

Iowa Property Laws and Drainage Changes

In Iowa, the landowner on the top of a hill has the right to let naturally-occurring water course down off his land to the neighbors, but the downhill neighbor has no duty to allow anything greater than the natural flow of water onto her property. What this means, unlike what some tile installers would have you believe, is that a downhill landowner has a say in an uphill owner's drainage operation. Property owners can't damn up water or dredge ditches and claim that the downhill result is a natural course. Making such changes removes your natural right to dump onto the lower ground.

The best way to avoid legal hassles is to amicably come to an agreement on **tile drain easements**. However, tile drain easements can come in a variety of forms, including:

- **Express Easements**: A written agreement for an easement that is recorded in the property records is called an *express easement*. Legally, it is probably the easiest easement to enforce.
- **Implied Easements**: An *implied easement* is one created by law, and the nature of an implied easement is determined by the nature of the property and its use.
    - For example, if you sold the back forty acres with a lane to it, but failed to mention the lane in the deed or other transfer paper work, it is implied that an easement exists on the lane, for access to the back forty.
- **Prescriptive Easements**: A prescriptive easement requires that you use land openly, for a period of time required by a state law.
    - For example, if you have been draining for more than 10 years, with no objection by the downhill owners, you likely have a *prescriptive easement* over the ground, even if a written, express easement hasn't been recorded.

2 ANIMALS

Animals are at the core of many, many farm operations, but even the grain farmer is likely to have a few animals or a farm dog around, and most anyone who farms is bound to encounter wild animals that impact the operation. The rules that affect animals cover a swath of farm life as varied as the animals themselves and the activities that involve them.

Dogs

A ***dog owner*** is liable for the action of his dog. Don't post "Beware of Dog" signs; believe it or not, if your dog was to ***injure someone***, such signs might be used against you in court, as an admission that you knew you were dealing with a problem animal. Your best advice is to ***control your animals***. You may ***kill*** a dog that is ***attacking or attempting to bite a human being***.

Every dog must have a ***rabies*** vaccination. Any dog, cat or other animal which has ***bitten or attacked*** a person must be ***reported.*** If rabies is suspected, animal-control officials can order the owner to ***confine*** the animal or it can be ***impounded*** by animal-control officials, who can hold the dog for ***ten (10) days*** and may then humanely destroy it. If the dog is returned to its owner, the owner must pay fees for impoundment.

> ***Note***: If you confine a non-livestock animal for suspected rabies (or any other reason), be aware that the Iowa Code makes it unlawful to "to fail to supply the animal during confinement with a sufficient quantity of food or water, or to fail to provide a confined animal with adequate shelter, or to torture, deprive of necessary sustenance, mutilate, beat, or kill such animal by any means which causes unjustified pain, distress or suffering."

It is **illegal to abandon** your pets or to allow them to run **loose**. Dogs under six months of age, and all other dogs that are wearing a collar with attached tags showing a valid rabies vaccination, along with the name and address of the animal's owner, are presumed to be someone's property. If these dogs are **impounded**, you must **claim them**, prove that they are current on **vaccinations**, and pay **impoundment fees** within **seven days**, or your dog could be destroyed.

Dogs not provided with a rabies vaccination tag are not presumed to be anyone's property. If a dog over six months of age is running loose and not wearing a valid rabies vaccination tag, it can be terminated by law enforcement.

If a stray dog is bothering your animals or livestock, **you may kill even a dog that is wearing a collar with a rabies vaccination tag** attached, when the dog is caught **in the act** of **chasing, maiming, or killing** any **domestic animal or fowl** (or when such a dog is attacking or attempting to bite a person). So, if your dog finds sport with the neighbor's flock of ducks, it may not be coming home.

> *Note: You have to kill the dog, while it is in the act. Shooting your neighbor's dog after it is done running your cattle through the fence is not allowed.*

Liability for Damages Caused by a Dog

The **owner** of a dog is **liable to an injured party** for all damages done by the dog, when the dog is caught in the action of worrying, maiming, or killing a domestic animal; or the dog is attacking or attempting to bite a person, except when the person damaged is doing an unlawful act, directly contributing to the injury. That means dogs biting people who are trespassing are not going to be in trouble.

You could also be held liable for damages to other property caused by your dog, if you allow it to run loose in violation of the law.

> *For example, if your neighbor complains about your loose dog, but you do nothing to restrain it, and it goes over again and digs up her newly-planted (and costly) rose bed and shrubs, you may have to pay to replace the plantings.*

Sales of Animals

Warranties

For the **purchase of trade animals**, a **warranty of fitness** is often either expressed or implied. An **express warranty** is one that is **stated or promised**. Examples of statements creating an express warranty, which **passes with title** to the animal, include promises made about the condition of an animal, like:

- "This heifer is open."
- "This bull is fertile."
- "These sheep are wormed."

If it turns out that the animal is not open, fertile, or wormed, then a **breach of warranty** may be found. If the defect is discovered before delivery, you can reject the shipment, but after accepting the delivery, the burden falls to the receiving party to **establish a breach** of warranty and to **seek damages** for it.

An **implied warranty** is one that is reasonably **assumed, under the existing circumstances**. For example, one would assume that the seller of a cat actually owns the cat that he or she is selling. If a buyer purchases the cat, with no knowledge of a **title defect** (i.e., no reason to think that the seller may not actually own the cat), then the buyer may prevail and receive damages, if some third party (the true cat owner) shows up and claims to have good title to the cat.

"**Puffing**" does not create a warranty. For example, "This goat will make you the top dog at your county fair," is not a warranty, but rather a puffing statement.

Payment for Animals Sold

The **Packers and Stockyard Act** ensures **timely payment** of funds for **animals sold**. It also regulates **stockyards**. If your farm operation contemplates **purchasing and grouping cattle** and then offering them for **resale** on a commission basis, you may be regulated by this federal law, which covers postings required and pricing rules.

Disposal of Dead Animals

Death loss is part of the livestock operation. You have the **right to dispose** of dead animals from your property that died on your property.

You can **bury, burn, or compost** the bodies of dead animals. The Department of Natural Resources has specific rules about **burial and covering** of animals you've disposed of, along with the **number of animal carcasses** that can be disposed of together, in one place. Any bodies not consumed by burning have to be covered in **quicklime** and buried **4 feet** or deeper **within 24 hours** of death.

Composting within 24 hours of death is also authorized, if:

- The animals are from your property;
- The remains are placed in a composter that is rot-resistant;
- The remains are placed outside of a floodplain on a hard surface; **and**
- The remains are covered with enough compost to prevent access by living animals.

The compost must be applied at a beneficial nutrient rate when the compost is removed.

Bees

You're required to **register your apiaries** with the **Farm Service Agency**, which can help avoid accidental damage to your hives by pesticide applications from other operations. In addition, all hive owners should **post a conspicuous sign** providing notice of where the beehives are and contact information, in order to protect them.

If you are applying pesticides to your own property and you have neighbors who keep bees, be aware of the damage that can be caused by **pesticide drift** from your operations. If the **label** on your pesticide indicates that it is **toxic to bees**, a **two-mile radius must be kept from any beehive registered with the FSA**; **or** if the application is to be **within the two miles**, you must provide the **beehive owner** with **at least 24 hours'** and **no more than 72 hours' notice of intent to spray**.

Wild Animals

Game Animals

Farmers are just like any other citizen, when it comes to the rules of the **Fish and Wildlife Division** of the Iowa DNR that protect **wild animals**. These rules include **game laws**, and a farmer must obey Iowa hunting rules for **game animals**. Even if the farm provides the lion's share of the food for most of the game animals in question, the farmer gets no special treatment.

Landowners have a right to **deer licenses** and a DNR program does allow **additional tags for crop damage**, but only if an agreement is executed with the DNR. Documentation is the key. Don't take matters into your own hands, without complying with the law.

Don't carry a loaded shotgun or other firearm in your combine – it's just a bad idea. Aside from the obvious potential for firearm accidents, you may be violating both **game laws** and **criminal laws**. Your combine is a **motor vehicle** and the rules that affect carrying firearms in motor vehicles apply to you, even though you are only going 5 mph.

Endangered Species

When it comes to animals that belong to an **endangered species**, most people know that you **cannot shoot, capture, or kill** one of them, but many are not aware that you **cannot modify the environmental situation or habitat** of an endangered species, which will have the effect of killing them. In fact, you are **never allowed to bait or kill** an endangered animal, even if it is killing your livestock.

If you accidentally **hit a wild animal with a vehicle**, and the animal you hit is a non-endangered game species, you may contact a DNR official for a "**salvage tag**" to harvest what is not embedded in your vehicle's grill.

Animal Nuisance Lawsuits

Unlike many other states, the law of **Iowa** provides **strong legal protection** for the unfettered **right to sue for nuisance**, where cause exists. A 1995 ruling from the Iowa Supreme Court made clear that in Iowa, the right to bring a nuisance lawsuit is a **constitutionally-**

protected property right, and the Court struck down an Iowa statute that would have prevented a landowner from bringing suit, on the basis that the statute was a "taking without just compensation" (a legal term employed mostly in cases where the state tries to zone property or to acquire it by eminent domain), which is prohibited by the 5th Amendment of the U.S. Constitution, applied to the states via the 14th Amendment.

Nuisance lawsuits are not uncommonly based on disturbances caused by ***animal feeding operations***. The Iowa DNR has extensive regulations and rules regarding animal feeding operations, and there are two things you need to know about the ***effect of state regulations on nuisance lawsuits***:

- ***Failure to comply*** with certain regulations may open you up to ***nearly automatic liability*** for nuisance; but
- ***Even full compliance*** with these regulations ***will not completely protect you*** from suit by adjoining landowners (although careful compliance with the regulations does at least appear to reduce the grounds on which plaintiffs may base nuisance claims).

Without this protection from suit, producers have been subjected to a number of lawsuits for a variety of reasons, including nuisance based on ***odor, bees' wings drift, noise, allegations that sulfur caused brain damage in an 18-year-old child, and contamination of underground oil reserves by animal waste***. However, ***hog confinements*** seem to be the real lightning rod for attracting nuisance actions.

Following state-required ***manure management plans*** and ***best industry practices*** helps, but it doesn't prevent these actions. ***Insurance***, which includes paying for the defense, can be purchased for producers who are engaged in hog production. Since the ***cost of defending*** one of these lawsuits often exceeds $100,000, you may consider insurance premiums to be cheap, by comparison.

Regulation of Animal Feeding Operations

The regulations of animal feeding operations is covered by over 162 pages of detailed ***Iowa state regulations***, contained in the Iowa

Administrative Code. The **basic definition of an animal feeding operation** is this:

> An **animal feeding operation** exists and is defined as a place where animals have been **stabled or fed for 45 days in a 12-month period and essential vegetation is not sustained** in the area.

This definition is also important, in determining whether you are a **"point source" of pollution**. If you meet the basic definition of animal feeding operation, and if you meet certain size and other qualifications, the federal EPA may determine that you meet the definition of a **Concentrated Animal Feeding Operation (or "CAFO")**, making your operation subject to **federal regulations**, as well.

Location of Animal Feeding Operations

The law regulates **separation distances** between the feedlot and **residences, churches, businesses, schools, public areas, water sources** and **environmental areas**. Further, operations cannot be situated in the **100-year floodplain**.

Size of Animal Feeding Operations

Size matters in the confined feeding world, because **exceeding certain numbers** of animals is **one way** (there are others, as explained below) to become **subject to regulation by the federal EPA as a "CAFO."** The chart below illustrates the numbers, for various types of animals, that will push you over this CAFO threshold:

Animal	Number of head
Dairy Cows	700
Veal Calves	1,000
Cattle	1,000
Swine over 55 lbs	2,500
Swine under 55 lbs	10,000
Horse	500
Sheep	10,000
Turkeys	55000

Hens or Broilers on liquid manure handling	30,000
Chickens non liquid manure handling	125,000
Laying Hens	82,000
Ducks if non liquid manure handling	30,000
Ducks on liquid manure handling	5,000

Even if you don't hit those above numbers, you can still be *regulated by the EPA as a "Medium CAFO," if*:

- You use a *ditch flushing system* or have *discharge directly into a stream*;
- You are found to be a *significant contributor of pollutants*; *and*
- You have the *numbers contained in the chart on the following page*:

Animal	Number of head
Dairy Cows	200-699
Veal Calves	300-999
Cattle	300-999
Swine over 55 lbs	750-2499
Swine under 55 lbs	750-9999
Horse	150-499
Sheep	3,000-9,999
Turkeys	16,500-54,999
Hens or Broilers on liquid manure handling	9,000-29,999
Chickens non liquid manure handling	37,500-124,999
Laying Hens	25,000-81,999
Ducks if non liquid manure handling	10,000-29,999
Ducks on liquid manure handling	1,500-4,999

Finally, a *"Small CAFO"* is an operation that has *fewer in number* than those above *but* has been *selected for regulation as a significant contributor of pollutants*.

Discharge of Water Pollutants

Under the federal *Clean Water Act,* discharge of water pollutants is regulated through the *National Pollutant Discharge Elimination*

System (NPDES). CAFOS that discharge or propose to discharge water pollutants may be required to obtain an **NPDES permit** from the EPA.

Before you ever begin discharging, you should determine **whether you need an NPDES permit**, and you should find out **how to avoid exceeding allowable discharge levels**. To determine whether your operation needs an NPDES permit, the operation will have to use an *assessment* based on its design. Sometimes a prior permanent fix or a precipitation-related discharge may avoid the need for a permit.

> **Note**: Getting the permit in advance avoids the penalty for not having one when it was needed, but obtaining a permit doesn't cure a situation in which you're going to have to pay a penalty for discharging in violation of what a permit would have allowed.

The EPA looks for and *penalizes* the *discharge* of a pollutant into a water of the United States **without a permit**, and to catch violators, the EPA uses *flyovers* in private small planes, especially after rains. They will also take reports from the disgruntled neighbor you outbid for his grandfather's farm property, when it auctioned.

EPA Enforcement Actions include warning letters, compliance orders, penalty orders (up to $177,500, at $16,500 per day) and judicial action (up to $37,500 per day with no max). Obviously, the consequences of failing to pursue the permit process or failing to comply by the terms of your permit can land you in some serious legal trouble, very quickly.

Confinement Operations

If you're thinking of operating a *confinement operation (an animal feeding operation entirely confined under a roof)*, you should seek legal help first. The *regulations* for confinement operations are complex, and again, the *penalties* for violations get expensive in a hurry.

Confinement operations that are considered "mid-size" or "large" are required to submit a *Manure Management Plan (MMP)* to the DNR, but an MMP is a good idea for any confined feeding operation. If you're also producing crops, an MMP is an excellent tool of efficiency, allowing you to optimize use of your own resources for crop production.

You must submit an MMP to the Iowa DNR, if your confinement feeding operation meets either of these criteria:

- The animal unit capacity is greater than 500 animal units and it was constructed or expanded after May 31, 1985; or
- The operation will have a manure storage structure and more than 500 animal units.

Note: *MMPS are also required if you plan to apply manure in Iowa that came from a non-Iowa confinement feeding operation with more than 500 animal units. MMPs need not be filed for open feedlots, unless they're necessary as a term of obtaining a permit from DNR or another agreement with the DNR.*

When it comes to efficient use of manure, an MMP helps you plan nutrient placement, by:

- Determining how much manure you produce;
- Pinpointing the nutrient concentration of manure;
- Identifying how many acres are necessary for land application; and
- Calculating how much manure is to be applied, per acre.

MMPs are developed using a phosphorus index. The idea is to base the application of manure on the maximum nitrogen needs of the crop, in specific application types and timing situations.

Note: *If you're spreading manure, be aware that most liquid manure must be spread at least 750 feet from neighbors, except if injected or incorporated, or if it comes from a small operation. Spreading manure close to neighbors is a great way to get your operation sued for nuisance, as well, and Iowa courts are not sympathetic to the spreader.*

Confinement operations must **store manure entirely between application periods**. Storage structure permits must be obtained from the DNR, with the submission of an MMP. It is interesting to note that an **MMP is required for storage facilities based on total capacity of the area**, not the amount in a building. **Even if the building is not in use**, a plan is still required to be on file, or proof of its decommissioning needs to be submitted to the DNR.

A ***Master Matrix***, which is a creature of state law, is administered by the ***County Board of Supervisors***, to ***score a potential confinement operation***, by assigning a potential operation points in various categories. In order to gain approval for a project, producers ***must pass 25 percent of the points in air quality, water quality, and community impact***. Once the matrix is submitted, the supervisors ***publish notice*** and have a ***public hearing***. The ***county takes a position***, and then the ***DNR evaluates*** the submission.

Specific matrix factors range the spectrum of issues that affect these operations, like where you are spreading or what type of structures are used. Much like the game of life, it is impossible to max out each category, but the matrix offers such a lengthy menu of options and selections, that a farmer will almost certainly be able to find a balance that will get the satisfactory score needed for approval of the project.

> *For example, a lack of points in some categories can be remedied, by obtaining extra points in others, as by choosing a site that exceeds the minimum required distances from protected buildings and areas or by installing extra odor-deterrence devices.*

An ***appeal*** is available to the Environmental Protection Commission, when the result you get is not satisfactory. The ***cost of the permit*** includes fees which fund an indemnity program for a ***disaster recovery*** event.

Veterinarians

Veterinarians provide a crucial service to any livestock operation, but vets are human, and they sometimes make mistakes. If you're disgruntled over a mistake made by your vet, and you think you'd like to sue him or her, you should consider the fact that you will face two main problems that commonly make ***veterinary malpractice cases*** unsavory for most plaintiffs:

- It is hard to find a veterinarian who will testify against another veterinarian (but you can be sure that every vet within 100 miles will find out that you sued a vet); and

- Animals are personal property. You usually cannot recover pain and suffering, or damages based on sentimental value. That takes the wind out of most cases right away.

If you're not dissuaded, then it's still up to you to prove veterinary malpractice. The burden of proof in a veterinary malpractice action is always on the plaintiff (which is what you are called, if you sue). In order to win, you'll have to be able to prove each of these things:

- A veterinarian's acts or omissions failed to meet the standard of care;
- Acts or omissions were negligently performed;
- Negligently performed acts or injuries caused the animal's injury or death; and
- As a result, the plaintiff was damaged.

The professional duty of a veterinarian usually begins with **obtaining a history of the animal** (which assistants can be used to develop) and a **physical examination**. The veterinarian is required to use professional learning, skill, and care, during the initial contact, the diagnosis of the problem, the decision and execution of treatment, and follow-up care.

In **obtaining permission for treatment**, there should be **disclosure of the risk of the treatment or drugs**. However, in one case where a horse died within 15 minutes of being injected with a drug, the court held that there was no duty to disclose or warn when the odds of a lethal outcome were 1 in 25,000.

The vet's act has to have **caused injury or death**. If you are calling a vet, the animal is likely sick already. You have to establish that the vet's act is the reason for the injury or death, not just that the steer died when the vet gave it a shot.

Other **miscellaneous considerations** that may be used against vets include:

- **Res ipsa loquitur.** This Latin phrase translates to, "the thing speaks for itself," and legally, it is used to mean that some mistakes are so obvious that the average person can figure out that the vet was responsible, without much further ado. Young lawyer wannabes are taught in law school that if you are *arguing* a res ipsa case for the injured party, you are arguing a loser.

- **Administrative Action for Malpractice.** A person may file an action against a veterinarian with the state administrative licensing board that oversees veterinarians. This action is not likely to result in compensation for damages to the complaining party unless clearly demonstrated.
- **Negligence.** If the actions in question are not within the realm of malpractice, then there may be common negligence. For example, if a veterinarian was overseeing the loading of a bull into a head gate and did not properly secure the head gate, the standard of care is that of regular negligence. Since you don't have to be a vet to load a bull into a gate, the claim would not be one for professional negligence, or malpractice.
- **"Bailment" Law.** When a veterinarian **boards** or **transports** animals, the vet is acting as a "*bailee*" of an animal, which may give a claim for negligent care of the animal while in custody. This is like when you give your coat to coat check. You aren't giving the coat away and you expect it to be returned in about the same condition that you gave it to them. In one case, an insured veterinarian was bailee of an elephant, "Sparkle," who died from poison while in his custody. A claim based upon a bailment does not require an expert witness, making it more practical and possibly cheaper to pursue. Again, just because the animal dies or is injured while in the custody of a vet doesn't make the vet liable for the death.

3 FARM PATENTS, COPYRIGHTS AND TRADEMARKS

Farmers are great inventors. Every year, they come up with thousands of great ideas to problems and make new ways to increase speed, efficiency and profitability. Many great inventors, however, have lost the profits from ideas stolen by nosy neighbors and overly observant package-delivery personnel. If you don't know how to legally protect your great idea, almost anyone can lift it and profit from your hard work.

A basic rule of thumb is not to share your idea with anyone, if you don't want someone jumping in on your potential fame and fortune. Instead, find an **intellectual property attorney**, a lawyer who handles patents, copyrights, trademarks, service marks, and trade secrets law. Get a nondisclosure agreement, and then get to work on cashing in.

What is Intellectual Property?

The term, **intellectual property,** also called **"IP,"** refers to an intangible, legal right to protect your ownership rights as the creator of a unique invention, the unique expression of an idea, or a unique business mark. Intellectual property law is extremely complex, and you genuinely need to consult a skilled IP lawyer, if you believe that you have invented something unique, which someone else might want to steal and profit from. Before you go to that first appointment, some basic terminology, taken from the **United States Patent and Trademark Office (USPTO)**, may help you understand some of the "patent-ese" that you'll be hearing from the attorney.

What Is a Patent?

A **patent** for an invention is the grant of ownership rights to the inventor, issued by the USPTO. Generally, the term of a patent is **20 years** from the date the application was filed.

A patent grants "the right to exclude others from making, using, offering for sale, or selling" the invention in the United States or "importing" the invention into the United States. What is granted is not the right to make, use, offer for sale, sell or import, but the right to exclude others from making, using, offering for sale, selling or importing the invention. Once a patent is issued, the government is done; you are on your own to protect your patent.

There are **three types of patents**:

1. **Utility patents** may be granted to anyone who invents or discovers any new and useful process, machine, article of manufacture, or composition of matter, or any new and useful improvement thereof;

   *The word "**process**" is defined as an act or method, and primarily includes industrial or technical processes. The term "manufacture" refers to articles that are made. The term "composition of matter" relates to chemical compositions and may include mixtures of ingredients, as well as new chemical compounds. These classes of subject matter taken together include practically everything that is made by man and the processes for making the products.*

2. **Design patents** may be granted to anyone who invents a new, original, and ornamental design for an article of manufacture; and
3. **Plant patents** may be granted to anyone who invents or discovers and asexually reproduces any distinct and new variety of plant.

Patent law specifies the general field of **subject matter** that can be patented and the conditions under which a patent may be obtained.

Usefulness

In every case, the subject matter (the thing you want to patent) must be "**useful**." The term "useful" refers to the condition that the subject matter has a useful purpose and also includes a requirement that the patent works. A machine that does not perform its intended purpose would not be called useful and will not be patented.

You can't patent laws of nature (gravity), physical phenomena (fire), or abstract ideas (freedom of speech); however, you may have copyrights in your own, unique **expression** of an idea (see below for more about copyrights). A patent cannot be obtained upon a mere idea or suggestion. The patent is granted upon the new machine, manufacture, etc. and not upon the idea or suggestion of the new machine. A complete description of the actual machine or other subject matter for which a patent is sought is required.

Novelty and Non-Obviousness

For an invention to be patentable, it must be **novel (new)**. An invention is **not new if:**

- The invention was known or used by others in this country, or patented or described in a printed publication in this or a foreign country, before the invention thereof by the applicant for patent; or
- The invention was patented or described in a printed publication in this or a foreign country or in public use or on sale in this country more than one year prior to the application for patent in the United States..."

If the invention has been described in a printed publication anywhere in the world, or if it was known or used by others in this country **before the date that the applicant made his or her invention**, a patent cannot be obtained. Likewise, if the invention has been described in a printed publication anywhere, or has been in public use or on sale in this country **more than one year before the date on which an application for patent is filed in this country**, a patent cannot be obtained. In this connection, it is immaterial when the invention was made, or whether the printed publication or public use was by the inventor or by someone else.

> *If the inventor describes the invention in a printed publication, uses the invention publicly, or places it on sale, he or she must apply for a patent before one year has gone by, or any right to a patent will be lost. However, in many foreign countries, the inventor must file on the date of public use or disclosure, in order to preserve patent rights.*

The subject matter for which a patent is sought must be sufficiently different from what has been used or described before, so that it may be said to be **nonobvious** to a person having ordinary skill in the area of technology related to the invention. For example, the substitution of one color for another or changes in size are ordinarily not patentable.

Seed Saving

Patented seeds are typically protected as **Utility Patents** or **Plant Patents**, which are both administered by the patent office and **allow the patent owner to exclude others from using them for 20 years**. Case law in the 1980s widened the scope of patentability to "anything under the sun that is made by the hand of man," including living organisms.

The main thing producers need to know is that, if you paid a premium for genetics, most likely the terms include an *agreement* that *prohibits you from saving seed*. The producers could be subject to random audit to show that the seed you planted yielded in the normal range and it was marketed or stored.

The *Plant Variety Protection Act*, administered by the **USDA**, offers a few **exemptions to the protections of the patent holder:**

- **Breeders or researchers** may be able to use the seed in *developing a new variety;*, and
- **Farmers** may be allowed to save seed for **replanting** if they **lawfully purchased** the seed.

The latter exemption does **not** give you the **right to resell the protected seed**, but only to replant for personal use, nor does it get you "off the plank" for purchasing unlawfully sold seed.

A **producer** can save **Public Varieties seed**. This seed can be saved, but public varieties are much more limited, as colleges follow the money trail and devote research budgets to genetically modified organism (GMO) traits. Plus, the public varieties do not have the yield potential and traits desired by most producers, who are attempting to beat razor-thin margins to remain profitable.

Look at the labels of the products you purchase, and **be wary of the ability to pick up GMO seed without having to pay a technology premium**. Better yet, just don't do it. Companies invest heavily in developing their products, and they are likely to invest heavily in defending their investments.

What Is a Trademark or Servicemark?

People have always liked to give their farms unique names. Maple Hill Farms, Here and There Farms, Sweet Valley Farms - the list goes on and on. Some of those farms have turned a name into marketing gold — Swiss Valley, Nieman Ranch, and Smuckers are just a few. Protecting that marketing gold with a servicemark or trademark is as important to a well-developed business plan as finding the capital to buy the golden goose.

A **trademark** is a **word, name, symbol, or device** that is used in trade with goods to **indicate the source of the goods** and to **distinguish** them from the goods of others. A **servicemark** is the same as a trademark except that it **identifies and distinguishes the source of a service** rather than a product. The terms, "trademark" and "mark" are commonly used to refer to both trademarks and servicemarks.

Trademark rights are used to prevent others from using a **confusingly similar mark**, but not to prevent others from making the same goods or from selling the same goods or services under a clearly different mark. Trademarks which are used in interstate or foreign commerce may be **registered** with the **USPTO**.

What Is a Copyright?

Copyright is a form of intellectual property protection provided to the authors of "**original works of authorship**," including literary, dramatic, musical, artistic, and certain other intellectual works, both published and unpublished, although any expression, once written down in unique form, qualifies for copyright protection. Copyright protection comes into being as soon as an expression is recorded in some manner – in writing, in audio recording, etc. These works may be registered with the USPTO, but they need not be, in order to be protected against plagiarism.

Generally, the law gives the owner of copyright the exclusive right to reproduce the copyrighted work, to prepare derivative works, to distribute copies of the work, or to publically perform or display the work.

The copyright protects the form of expression, rather than the subject matter of the writing. A description of a machine could be copyrighted, as could photographs taken of the machine once built, but this would only prevent others from copying the exact description or using your photographs without permission; it would not prevent others from writing a description of their own or from making and using the machine.

For example, a book describing a feeding nutrition system would be copyrightable, but the actual feeding system would likely not be covered by a copyright. It would be best subject to a patent as a useful, non-obvious process.

Marketing materials, like advertisements for farm products, also receive copyright protection of both the text and the photographs or videos used, preventing others from exactly duplicating your unique advertisements.

4 BANKRUPTCY

Bankruptcy is a federal creation designed to allow people and businesses who meet certain criteria to discharge (or remove) their obligation to pay debts they have incurred. You've probably heard about bankruptcies being filed under one or another of the various Bankruptcy Code "chapters," and each chapter has a unique set of requirements, standards, rules, and obligations that it imposes on debtors and on creditors who want to file claims. Generally speaking, farm businesses can file under Chapter 7 (Liquidation), Chapter 12 (Farm Re-organization), or Chapter 13 (Re-organization) of the Bankruptcy Code.

Bankruptcy Definitions

Before you learn more about the different chapters of the Bankruptcy Code, here are a few general definitions you'll need to understand first:

A ***debtor*** is a person who owes money to some person or entity.

A ***creditor*** is a person or entity to which money is owed by a debtor.

A ***secured creditor*** is a creditor that has loaned money to a debtor, in exchange for the debtor's agreement that certain property belonging to the debtor (like a house, a car, a tractor, or a savings account) will stand as collateral, to ensure repayment of the loan. To qualify as a secured creditor, a creditor must meet certain formalities. You are only a secured creditor if you have filed correct filing statements with the Iowa Secretary of State.

> *For example, if you sell a tractor over time to your neighbor, and you file proper forms, you are a **secured creditor**. If you*

just lent money to someone without filing the paperwork, you are an **unsecured creditor**.

A **bankruptcy trustee** is someone appointed by the bankruptcy court to supervise the action and find assets to sell, so that proceeds can be sued to pay creditors.

The **bankruptcy estate** is all of the debtor's assets and possessions at the time of filing.

Chapter 7 Bankruptcy - Liquidation

A **Chapter 7 bankruptcy** is a **liquidation** bankruptcy. The ultimate intended result in a Chapter 7 bankruptcy is to gather all of the debtor's **assets** into a **bankruptcy estate**, determine which assets are **exempt** from liquidation, sell any assets that are **non-exempt**, and use the funds to make payments against the debts owed to **creditors.**

The **debtor** files a **statement of assets and debts** with the court. Notice is given to **creditors**, who file **claims** with the court, stating how much is owed to them. The debtor asks the court to order those debts **non-payable** by the filing debtor.

The debtor gets to retain a list of **"exempt" property** for the debtor's **"fresh start."** In Iowa, this generally means

- The first $10,000 of **tools** of the trade;
- The first $40,000 of **equity** (meaning non-mortgaged value) in a house;
- $1,000 **cash** in a bank account or
- Any interest in IRAs/401Ks;
- The first $7,000 of value in a **vehicle** (again, the portion of the vehicle not covered by a loan);
- One **rifle** and one **shotgun**; and
- $7,000 of value in **household goods**.

Any assets over that amount (for example, campers, ATVs, and snowmobiles) may be taken by the trustee and sold. The proceeds from the sale are then split between the trustee (who takes 25 percent) and all of the creditors of the debtor. This usually results in creditors receiving pennies on the dollar owed.

The debtor is then **discharged** from any further obligation to pay most general debts. Certain debts, including back taxes owed and child support obligations owed, are not dischargeable in bankruptcy.

Chapter 13 Bankruptcy – The "Wage Earner's" Plan

Chapter 13 bankruptcy is a **reorganization** of debt and a court-supervised attempt (the plan) to pay debts of the debtor over time. Chapter 13 is also known as the **"wage earner's plan."** The ultimate goal is to **stop collection activity**, and give a **working debtor** who has **regular income** an opportunity to **repay debts at an affordable rate**.

In a Chapter 13 bankruptcy case, a debtor develops a detailed repayment plan allowing him to pay creditors' claims, using projected future earnings, over the course of **three-to-five years**. During this time, creditors may not undertake collection efforts. Some debts can be reorganized, sometimes against the creditors' wishes, and creditors are placed in different classes, who are paid differently under the plan.

When a Chapter 13 is filed, the **repayment plan** is filed with it. The bankruptcy court must approve your plan, but **payments must start within 30 days of filing**, even if the plan is not yet approved.

There are two things you should know about Chapter 13 bankruptcy, before you decide to file one:

- **Filing a Chapter 13 bankruptcy costs a lot more than a Chapter 7.** Due to its complexity and the time it takes to complete a three-to-five year case, Chapter 13 generates much higher legal fees and other expenses.
- **Chapter 13 plans often fail.** It is very common for Chapter 13 plans to fail, because financial ability to make the payments dips when the debtors get divorced, lose their income, or experience other unexpected pitfalls, during the three-to-five-year plan period.

Many people file Chapter 13 because they have too much equity in a home or some other asset with a secured debt, and they do not want to give it up for liquidation in a Chapter 7, even when they are being smothered by other debts, like medical bills and credit cards, that could be fully discharged in a Chapter 7. It is true that you can keep more assets in a Chapter 13, if you are successful in fulfilling your plan obligations.

Debtors who are unsuccessful in Chapter 13 cases wind up **converting** their bankruptcies to Chapter 7, after paying out a great deal of money on plan payments and fees. Often, it is better to be pragmatic from the start, let go of the homestead, and save all that money to use for moving on.

Chapter 12 Bankruptcy – Farm Reorganization

A **Chapter 12 bankruptcy** is a form of Chapter 13 bankruptcy, with **special farm provisions**, intended to help farmers reorganize and carry out a **repayment plan** to make installment payments to creditors over **three-to-five years**, with five being the max and three being the preferred.

> *Chapter 12 is more streamlined, less complicated, and less expensive than Chapter 11, which is aimed towards large corporate reorganizations, but many farmers may not find Chapter 13 to be a good fit for their financial needs, because it is designed for those who have smaller debts than a farm could be facing.*

You cannot be forced to file a Chapter 12 proceeding, like you can be in Chapter 7, 11, and 13. In Chapter 12, **creditors don't have the right to approve your plan** like they do in a Chapter 11. You **must have permission to get rid of assets** if you are in a Chapter 12. If you want to do that, you need to provide the creditor **"adequate protection"** to ensure that the creditor is not left out in the cold.

Eligibility for Chapter 12 Bankruptcy

Farmers eligible for Chapter 12 must be either:

- An **individual** or **individual and spouse**; or
- A **corporation** or **partnership**.

Individuals must meet each of the following **four Chapter 12 requirements:**

1. The individual or husband and wife must be **engaged in a farming operation**;

2. The **total debts** (secured and unsecured) of the operation must be **not over $3,792,650**;
3. At least **half of the total debts** that are fixed in amount (not including debt on the house) must be **related to farming**; **and**
4. More than **half of the gross income** of the individual or the husband and wife for the preceding tax year or for each of the second and third prior tax years must have been earned **from farming**.

A **corporation or partnership** must meet the following **Chapter 12 eligibility requirements** (as of the date of the **filing** of the petition):

- **Over one-half of the outstanding stock or equity** in the corporation or partnership must be **owned by one family** or by one family and its relatives;
- The **family** or the family and its relatives **must conduct the farming**;
- **Over 80 percent** of the value of the corporate or partnership **assets** must be related to the **farming or fishing operation**;
- The **total indebtedness** of the corporation or partnership must be **not over $3,792,650**;
- At least **half** of the corporation's or partnership's **total debts** which are fixed in amount (excluding debt on one home occupied by a shareholder) must be **related to farming**; **and**
- If the corporation issues stock, the **stock cannot be publicly-traded**.

Chapter 12 contains a **special automatic stay provision** that protects **co-debtors**. Unless the bankruptcy court orders it, a creditor may not collect a **"consumer debt"** from **any individual who also owes a debt jointly with the debtor**. Consumer debts are those incurred by an individual primarily for a personal, family, or household purpose.

Your Farm as a Creditor

Your operation may find itself in the position of a creditor, rather than a debtor, when someone who owes you money files bankruptcy. In order to seek repayment in this situation, there are certain things you need to do. Here are answers to a few common questions you might have:

How do I protect my custom farm operation from people filing bankruptcy against it?

The simple solution is to get payment at the time you perform the service. If you round bale, collect the payment per bale before the bales leave the field. Not only will you not have a dispute about how many bales are made, but you will not serve as a short-term lender to the person who hired you.

You can file a custom farm lien against a farm for work performed, but in the event of a bankruptcy, from a practical standpoint, you may move yourself to the front of the line, only to receive little income.

How do I protect my operation once I receive Notice of Bankruptcy from someone who owes me money?

Stop contacting them at once. Don't send anymore statements and don't call them about their debts. The bankruptcy court issues an ***"automatic stay,"*** a court order that halts any attempts to collect a debt, once the debtor files.

If you have ***secured debt***, you ***can*** contact the debtor to see if they want to ***"reaffirm"*** their debt. This means that the debtor indicates that, despite the bankruptcy filing, it wants to keep the property. In exchange, the debtor has to continue to pay the debt. If the debtor doesn't want to pay the debt, the debtor can ***abandon*** the property. If your secured debtor abandons the property securing the debt owed to you, you can go ***retrieve*** the property, but you cannot seek any additional funds from the debtor.

What if they come in to pay anyway?

If someone files a bankruptcy against a debt they owe you, and then returns to your place of business and attempts to pay you for it anyway, things change. This is called a ***reaffirmation*** of the debt, and once they pay on it or state they will pay on it despite the bankruptcy, the debt is no longer non-payable and you may take funds from the debtor.

How do I Deal with Bad Checks?

If you are a presented a check that is returned for nonsufficient funds, you have turned into an ***unplanned creditor***. The first step is to call the check issuer and then the bank that the check is issued on.

The bank will frequently indicate whether or not the check would be honored, if it were presented again. Sometimes, it is just a matter of timing.

If not, you should have the check presented again. After its **second dishonor**, you need to send a **notice** to the check writer that, if it is not honored within **ten (10) days**, you will turn it into the local law enforcement for pursuit as a **theft charge**. This notice should be by **registered mail or personally served** by someone other than you.

Each local enforcement district has slightly different standards on what they want you to include when you turn it over for a theft charge, so check in advance with the agency to make sure you are set up for success.

> **NOTE**: If you take checks that are **postdated**, **third-party** checks, or those intended for **loan payments**, dishonor by the bank will generally not be pursued by law enforcement as theft charges.

When you contact someone who owes you money, **never** make **threats**, contact their **relatives**, harass them at **work** or continue to contact them **at all after** he or she indicates that he or she represented by an **attorney** (contact the attorney, instead).

5 CONTRACTS

Contracts are made all the time, and no one really stops to think about them, until one goes bad. That's when you need to peel apart the equation, to determine:

- Has an enforceable contract been formed?
- If so, what damages or compensation may be available?

Forming Enforceable Contracts

Whether a contract is written or oral (verbal), a contract is formed according to a simple math equation: **Offer** plus **Acceptance** and **Consideration**, with **Capacity**, equals **Contract**.

*For example, assume Ida has the **capacity** to make a contract (meaning she is over 18 and not drunk or under duress). When Ida says to you, "I would like to offer you $1,650 for your Oliver 77," she has simply made an **offer**. In order for an enforceable contract to be formed, there must be more. Suppose you say, "Yes," and Ida hands you a check. Then, we have a contract, as you have **accepted** and Ida has provided **consideration** (something of value).*

The Offer

In dissecting the offer, the offer must be seen as **reasonable** and made with a **serious** intention. The subject-matter of the contract must be **not illegal**.

*For example, offering to sell your children is generally taken as neither serious nor reasonable(even if it was taken seriously, it would be **automatically unreasonable** as **illegal** and thus, **voidable**).*

The terms of an offer should be both **certain** and **definite**, such as price per part with delivery on a specific day. Advertisements are generally too vague to be considered offers. They are invitations to deal.

The offer must be actually **communicated** to the other party. Until the other side **accepts**, you can withdraw your offer, unless your offer stated that it would be open for a specific period of time. If you never hear from the other side, your offer is still considered to be withdrawn after a **reasonable** amount of time has passed. Rewards are offers that lapse after a rational amount of time (finding a lost kitten two years after a "reward" flyer was posted does not get you the $20 reward).

Offers are also considered withdrawn, if the offer-maker **dies** or the offer cannot happen because performance of the contract becomes **impossible**.

> For example, you offer to rent a grain bin, but a tornado removes the grain bin. Your offer to rent it has been extinguished, as performance is now impossible.

Acceptance

Acceptance is pretty simple. If you indicate you **agree**, you have accepted. **Silence** is not acceptance, but if someone offers to combine your corn for $1,000 and you watch them do it without stopping them, your silence in that situation is really considered **non-verbal conduct**, indicating that you agree, by allowing performance, which is the same as agreeing.

Consideration

Consideration is **anything of value**, any amount of anything to secure the deal. In real estate, it is referred to as "**earnest money**."

Even the mere promise to act or not to act can be consideration adequate to form a valid contract. An interesting concept in contracts is that the actual money does not have to be in hand, in order for there to be consideration. The mere promise to pay is held to have value, and therefore, the promise to pay can create an enforceable obligation to pay. In fact, most contracts are formed when mutual promises are made – before anything else actually changes hands.

Capacity

Doogie Howser, MD, might save lives, but he couldn't contract to order the toilet seat covers at his hospital. Why? Because he is **underage**. Being a minor is considered to be an **incapacity,** and if you make a contract with a minor, the kid can revoke your contract at any time. As long as the minor who revokes a contract leaves the other party in the same position as they were before the contract, no damages can be sought.

> *For example, if you're thinking about selling that 756 IHC to that 16-year-old kid from the FFA, get a parent to sign the purchase contract; otherwise, you risk having the tractor show back up after planting time.*

Legally insane or **drunk persons** also lack capacity to enter valid contracts. A **person without authority to bind another** lacks capacity to enter into a contract on behalf of that other.

> *For example, your neighbor can't decide to sell your tractor to either the 16-yr-old FFA kid or to his parents, unless you have given your neighbor* **authority** *(like a power of attorney) to enter that contract on your behalf.*

Authority can also come through the terms of **employment contracts**. For example, an international buyer for a huge department store may have authority to purchase goods, but a store clerk may not (otherwise, the world's least favorite corporations might be stuck buying lots of goods they didn't want). A lack of authority to bind someone else to purchase something is also the reason why, despite high-school pranks, like filling out dozens of magazine subscription cards in the principal's name, the school administrator will not be stuck paying for a five-year Cosmo subscription.

Mistakes

If one side makes a **mistake** and it is **material (important) to the contract**, that side is out of luck. On the other hand, if there is a **mutual mistake** (if both sides have made a mistake), the contract is **voidable** (the people can decide not to perform the contract).

> For example, if you hire someone to drill in soybeans, and you wanted them in 20-inch rows, not 30, but you didn't mention that to the custom operator, you are likely stuck with the 30-inch rows that resulted from your **unilateral mistake**. You get a different result, when you order a 25 horsepower tractor, the dealer sells you a 25 horsepower tractor, but a 45 horsepower tractor is delivered. You do not get to keep the more expensive tractor, because it is a **mutual mistake** of the parties.

Substantial Performance of a Contract

Substantial performance is a legal doctrine in contract law that essentially means that "close enough" counts. If the majority of the contract performance has already been completed by one party to the contract, then the other party is stuck having to perform its side.

> For example, consider a situation in which you ordered a new Case tractor, in white, to match your fleet of white Case Agri Kings. When the Case IH tractor shows up, but it is red, you may likely be stuck with it.

Auction Sales

An **auctioneer** works for the seller, as the **seller's agent**. The seller picks the auctioneer, is paid by the auctioneer, and the auctioneer will not sell, if that's what the seller wants done. If the auctioneer, as agent for the seller, exceeds the **authority** given to him by the seller, the buyer cannot bind the seller to perform.

> For example, if a seller hires an auctioneer for the limited purpose of auctioning household items located inside the home of the seller's dearly-departed grandparents, but the auctioneer also auctions off family-heirloom items that were previously moved to a storage building way out back, the winning bidders on the heirloom items cannot force the seller to sell them under those terms.

A bid is an offer to buy. If an auction is conducted **with reserve**, the auctioneer can reject all bids. In a **non-reserve** auction, the highest bidder wins, regardless. A winning bidder may not be bound to follow through with the purchase, if either the seller or the auctioneer has made **material, fraudulent representations** about the property being sold. **Puffing** by the auctioneer is acceptable, but fraud is not.

Production Contracts

A **production contract** can be defined as an agreement under which a **producer agrees** to **raise** a **commodity** in a manner established by the contractor and to **deliver** the commodity to the contractor; while the **contractor agrees to pay** the producer, in return.

A *"commodity"* can include *livestock, raw milk, and crops.*

"**Livestock**" includes beef cattle, dairy cattle, sheep, and swine.

"Crops" include plants used for food, animal feed, fiber, or oil, if the plant is classified as a forage or cereal plant. This includes, but is not limited to, alfalfa, barley, buckwheat, corn, flax, forage, millet, oats, popcorn, rye, sorghum, soybeans, sunflowers, wheat, and grasses used for forage or silage, but not plants produced to create seed for sale.

Production Contract Liens

What if the contractor refuses to pay, after the commodity has been grown and delivered? One inexpensive way that producers can reduce their risk is by filing a **commodity production contract lien**.

If you are contracted to produce a commodity, you can file a production lien. The amount of the lien is equal to the amount owed to you, pursuant to the terms of the production contract. The lien applies to the actual product produced or the proceeds from sale of the products.

A producer *"perfects"* a commodity production contract lien by filing a *financing statement* with the *Secretary of State*, within *45 days* of the livestock's *arrival* or the date when the crop is *planted*.

> **Note:** If the contract provides for **continuous arrival** of livestock, the producer must file within **180 days** of the livestock's **arrival**.

Custom Feeding Arrangements

One type of contract farm operations are seeing more and more is a **custom feeding contract**. Any feeding contract should make provisions for *(1) handling and feeding, (2) division of profit or loss*, and *(3) marketing of the livestock*. The contract should state the approximate **delivery date** and **deadline for delivery**. **Shrink** needs to be addressed, especially if rate of gain is used to determine any type of payment. **General management practices** and expectations should be written and agreed upon and provisions should be made for **repossession** of livestock that is not cared for properly.

Generally, the feeder is responsible for the proper manure handling, storage, and liability. The agreement should include the type and weight of animal to be fed. The owner and feeder both know the approximate time of marketing and desired state at marketing and how shipping is paid for. A clause should be included for low-performing animals and allow for their early departure.

Some feedlots will **finance** the **feed bill** for customers, and some will finance the **cattle**. However, it is not uncommon for the feedlot operator to require a **deposit upon delivery**. The deposit will be applied to overall expenses. Interest rates vary and are usually based off the prime rate.

When cattle are fed under contract, the owner retains **title** to the cattle. The **risk of loss** due to **death** is usually borne by the **owner**, except for those death losses caused by **negligence of the feeder**. Death losses will usually be borne by the owner. The parties also have the option of agreeing to **share losses**, above a certain percentage of dead. This has problems as only one party will be around to verify the death loss. Both parties need to determine whose insurance company will cover losses due to **catastrophe** like fire, wind and lighting.

Feeding is central to the operation. Don't forget to consider the following aspects of any contract feed arrangement:

Ration composition. The feedlot should provide cattle owners with a report of the ration composition. This report should include not only the amounts of each feedstuff but also a report on the total ration's energy, protein and major vitamins and minerals. A list of feed additives should also be included. Knowing where the feedlot gets its feeding program and if they pay timely is often a key to understanding the nature of the operation you are dealing with.

Cost of feed charged by the feedlot. Feed may be marked up to cover overhead costs. Some agreements mark up the feed a little and do not charge "yardage." Others may charge a little more for yardage and not mark up the feed. Find out how both parties think this is going to work. The yardage fee will vary from lot to lot. Some charge a yardage fee and some don't. The important thing is to ask.

The two most common ways of charging for services are yardage or yardage plus feed markup. Yardage is usually charge on a dollar/head/day basis. In yards that have a higher yardage charge, the feed markup is generally less. Cost of arrival treatments usually includes cost of vaccination, de-wormer, implants, etc. Labor cost may or may not be included in the yardage charge. The feedlot operator should send a complete record of the delivered feed and its cost. Billings should reflect changes in ration ingredient cost. The bill should contain an itemized list of any other costs billed to the cattle owner. The first bill should state the cost of processing. If the feed is financed through the feedlot, look for a statement of interest on the bill. It is a good idea to specify with the feedlot the exact time when interest charges for feed begin to accrue.

Tax consequences. Because feed prices can change, some feedlots allow customers to ***prepay*** for some or all of the feed. The key point to keep in mind is that ***IRS regulations*** do not allow one to pay a ***true feed bill*** in advance of its purchase and take a deduction, but the IRS allows the purchase of commodities such as grain, silage, or hay for future use to be deducted. Check with your tax preparer about ***prepaying commodities*** if you are feeding cattle into the next year.

6 FARM TRANSPORTATION ISSUES

As farms become larger and equipment follows along, operations frequently find themselves under the watchful eye of the state and federal Departments of Transportation (DOT), along with other agencies, like the Environmental Protection Agency (EPA) and its state counterparts. Farm operations need to beware of and follow applicable regulations or face stiff penalties that can quickly wipe out any benefits gained from operating large equipment.

Definitions and General Rules

In order to understand many DOT regulations, you should keep in mind a few, basic definitions that are used frequently in those regulations, to characterize or identify various farm vehicles:

- **Tractor:** A vehicle designed primarily as a farm implement for drawing plows, mowing machines and other implements of husbandry.
- **Grain Cart:** A vehicle with a single or tandem non-steerable axle, designed to move grain.
- **Implement of Husbandry**: A vehicle manufactured, designed, or reconstructed for agricultural purposes and used exclusively in the conduct of ag operations.

If you plan to hit the public roadways driving any one of these vehicles, a few basic rules apply to all of them.

Necessary Equipment

Each farm vehicle must be operated at *less than 35 mph* on roads. In addition, the vehicle must have a *slow-moving vehicle device* and *amber flashing lights* from sunset to sunrise. These implements must be *able to yield half of the road*.

If you're towing something, then a **safety chain** is required between the power source and the first towed piece if the power source is *not* a tractor. *No more than three* vehicles (power plus two) are allowed. At night, you need a solid *red taillight on the trail vehicle* and a *flashing amber light*, if the flashing light from the power source cannot be seen.

Slow-Moving Vehicles

Slow-moving vehicles include all animal-drawn vehicles, implements of husbandry, and other machinery *designed* for operation at a speed of *30 miles per hour or less.* When they are operated on the public roadways, each one of these vehicles *must display a triangular slow-moving vehicle emblem*, which consist of a *fluorescent or illuminated red-orange triangle* with a *dark red reflective border* and be mounted so as to be *visible* from a distance of not less than *600 feet to the rear*.

No other vehicles are permitted to display this device. However, *towed implements of husbandry* that are *empty* and *not self-propelled* can be towed at lawful speeds over 30 miles per hour, without removing the slow-moving vehicle emblem.

> **Note:** As long as the primary power unit towing an implement of husbandry or other machinery displays a slow-moving vehicle sign that is *visible from a distance of 600 feet to the rear*, it is not necessary to display another sign on the towed unit.

Weight

As a general rule, the more axles and the more length you have, the more weight you are allowed to haul. Just like in gym class, however, the more you weigh, the more attention you are likely to receive from the authorities.

Essentially, vehicles are broken down by the following weight classes

- **10,000** pounds and under
- **26,000** pounds and under
- **96,000** pounds and under.

As you will see throughout this chapter, different DOT regulations apply to vehicles in each of these weight categories. Since the penalties for violating transportation safety regulations can be stiff, you should ensure that you are complying with the rules, before you ever hit the road in your farm vehicle. When in doubt, seek a professional opinion from the state or federal DOT or consult an attorney.

Driver Qualifications

Drivers Licenses

Under state and federal laws, the **type** of vehicle you operate, **where** you operate it, and **what** you're doing with it, determines the **type of drivers license** you need. In general, you are exempt from any driver's licensing requirements (i.e., you don't even need an ordinary drivers license), while **driving a farm tractor or implement of husbandry to and from the home farm buildings to any adjacent or nearby farmland for farming purposes**.

> *For example, having your 14-year-old move the tractor from the home farm down the road to grandma's is legal (although you'll have to decide whether it's wise), but letting her drive it to school for FFA week is not.*

Under **Iowa DOT law**, farm drivers who stay **within the state** are **exempt** from age, medical fitness, and hours of service requirements – all **special licensing requirements** that the DOT imposes on other operators. These exemptions are lost when you cross a state line, transport cargo for hire or transport nonfarm cargo.

> *For example, you and your sister transport your own produce to sell in a farmer's market that is part of a larger flea market going on in the next county. At that point, you're exempt from special licensing requirements, because you're within your own state, transporting **farm cargo**. However, when your sister persuades you to return with a trailer full of her Amish furniture purchases, you're transporting **non-farm cargo**, and you're no longer exempt. The same is true if you're persuaded to transport your aunt's household goods or any other non-farm cargo*

FIELD MANUAL

Under USDOT law, operators within **150 air miles** of their farm, **regardless of state lines**, are exempt from the driver requirements. If you're **not exempt**, you must obtain a **USDOT number**.

Both your USDOT number and your operating name must be displayed on both sides of the machinery. The display must be legible, with sharp contrasting color, and visible in the daylight from 50 feet away, when stationary.

To obtain the number, call (800) 832-5660, or go to www.fmcsa.dot.gov.

Driver License Requirements

Vehicle	Weight	License w/I 150 air miles	License past 150 air miles
Pickup	10,000 or under	C	C
Pickup	26,001+ and trailer 10,001+	C	A (CDL)
Truck Tractor	26,001+	D1	A (CDL)
Truck Tractor and Trailer		D1	A(CDL)
Straight Truck	26,001+	C	B (CDL)
Straight Truck	16,001-26,000	C*	C*

* Farmers are exempt from D license requirement

Medical Certification Cards

Those who hold certain types of drivers licenses must carry **medical cards**, certifying that they've had appropriate physicals to determine that they do not suffer from health conditions that could making driving larger vehicles dangerous. As long as you stay **within the state of Iowa** or go **no more than 150 air miles away from your home farm**, even if you cross state lines, you do **not** need a **medical**

card. Air miles are determined by a circle on a map, not how many miles your GPS says it takes to drive to a point via roads.

> *Depending on what state you cross into, this may be a problem regardless of what Iowa says. The best practice is to stay in your home state.*

Business-Trade Trucks

To obtain ***business-trade truck tags***, Iowa law requires you to certify that the business is the only use of the truck, and then you must ensure that the truck is used for nothing else. The ***penalty for false registration*** is currently $2,250, and 25 percent of that fee stays with the county treasurer. That is of note because it provides an incentive to the county to question and pursue those who seek to abuse the system.

Qualifying a vehicle as a business-trade truck under Iowa law can offer tax and other benefits. In order to qualify, the truck must be:

- ***Eligible for depreciation*** under IRS rules; and ***either***
    - Owned by a corporation, LLC, Partnership, or a sole proprietor who files a tax schedule F or C; ***or***
    - Leased by a corporation, LLC, partnership, or sole proprietor, ***and*** used primarily for business or farming operations.

> ***Note***: *While it may be tempting to use the crew cab truck to haul the kids to the river for a boat ride, hauling a boat with business trade plates on your truck is asking for an "education session" with the DOT, and the "tuition" for this schooling will likely be a steep fine.*

A weight/value formula is used to determine the licensing fees for 2010 and newer trucks under 10,000 pounds, cars, and SUVs.

Transporting Raw Agricultural Products

When in ***Iowa***, trucks or combinations ***transporting raw agricultural products*** are allowed to operate in excess of their *registration weight* by up to **25 percent**, but are **not over the maximum gross weight** listed in the wheelbase tables. This allowance is not valid outside of Iowa.

Things considered to be **raw farm products** include **ag lime, fresh vegetables, peat, threshed potatoes, corn cobs, grain (excluding cracked or ground grain or soybean meal, unless being transported directly to the farm from the processor), raw dairy products, dead animals, hair, raw milk, baled or loose hay, saw logs, eggs, fresh or frozen hides, separated cream, firewood, honey, flax, honeycomb, sod, flax seed, live poultry, soil, fertilizer, fodder, livestock, soybeans, fresh berries, melons, baled or loose straw, fresh fruit, nursery stock, and wool.**

Once something has been processed, it is no longer a "raw agricultural product." However, **processed grain** may still qualify for the **25 percent registration weight tolerance**, if it is transported to the place of processing and **immediately returned** to the farm after processing. A **processing receipt** is required on the return trip to qualify for the weight tolerance. A good rule of thumb to remember is that if you smash it, grind it, cook it or distill it, it is likely no longer raw.

Bridge Limits

All **trucks weighing more than 80,000 lbs (40 tons)** have to comply with **posted weight limits on bridges**. Fence line feeders, grain carts, tank wagons and tracked implements are all subject to bridge embargoes and weight laws.

Truck Inspections

All vehicles 10,001 pounds or heavier must be inspected annually. When traveling in these trucks, you must either have an inspection decal visible on the vehicle or keep the inspection sheet available to prove that the truck has been inspected.

> *Consider picking a date and insuring that the inspections are done for all vehicles on that date. Talk with the local inspectors to determine when is a smart time to get the inspections, preferably at a time when your demand on the vehicle is low.*

ATVs and the Road

ATVs can be driven on the road, by persons with a ***valid driver's license***, but only under one of these ***conditions***:

1. Between ***sunrise and sunset*** for use connected to ***agriculture***, including fueling yourself (with food) and fueling the vehicle.
2. When used by a licensed ***engineer*** for ***surveying***.
3. ***Government*** use of ATV for utility, emergency or DNR work.
4. In the right-of-way at least five feet from the edge of ***your own property (or your family's)***, but not alongside an interstate or other restricted-access highway.

Fuel Storage Issues

Farms vehicles use a lot of fuel, and most farms store fuel for rapid access and to control price. ***Fuel storage tanks*** are subject to a variety of strict rules that must be followed carefully, if you want to avoid having legal claims brought against your farm. Following fuel storage tank rules also protects your farm from the possible denial of an insurance claim, if disaster strikes. All tanks must be ***UL approved***, have an ***external gate valve***, ***check valves***, and ***proper venting***. Additionally, they should be ***placed*** at least ***40 feet away from buildings*** and ***100 feet downslope from wells***.

Here are some additional rules that apply to specific types of fuel storage tanks:

- ***Tanks with capacity over 1,100 gallons*** must be registered with the state fire marshal, have a secondary containment plan, and obey any local fire jurisdiction rules.
- ***Underground tanks*** with ***more than 1,100 gallons*** must have an annual tag attached to the file pipe. If they have less than 1,100 gallons of capacity, a permanent tag is required.

Spills, Prevention, and Containment

Farms that began operation after ***August 16, 2002*** must have ***written spill-prevention plans*** for all ***above-ground oil and fuel storage***, detailing how they will ***prevent, handle, and clean up any spills***. Actually, according to the EPA, farms that began operation before August 16, 2002 were required to have the spill prevention plans from 1972, when the Clean Water Act was passed, though that has never been enforced.

While plan requirements vary (see below), **farms that meet these three requirements have to have a plan in place:**

- The farm stores, transfers, uses, or consumes **oil or oil products**, such as diesel fuel, gasoline, lube oil, hydraulic oil, adjuvant oil, crop oil, vegetable oil or animal fat;
- The farm can **reasonably expect to discharge oil or fuel into waters of the U.S.**; and,
- The farm stores **more than 1,320 gallons** in **above-ground** containers

The 1,320 gallon above-ground container count does not include the capacity of tractors, combines or trucks or other mobile equipment or pesticide application containers, or mixing tanks or milk bulk tanks and pipes. It does include the capacity of any containers more than 55 gallons that store diesel fuel, gasoline, lube oil, hydraulic oil, adjuvant oil, crop oil, vegetable oil, or animal fat.

> *Every farm operation uses oil products. And while you can attempt to demonstrate an exemption because you can't have a spill into a water of the U.S., that definition is under constant attack. The better course of action is to comply if you have over 1,320 gallons in above ground containers.*

Spill Prevention Plan Requirements

- If your farm's **combined above-ground oil and fuel storage totals more than 10,000 gallons**, you must have a **professional engineer** prepare a spill prevention plan.
- If you store **between 1,320 and 10,000 gallons** ((as long as no single container holds over 5,000 gallons **and** you have no history of major spills), you can use an EPA template to **self-certify your compliance**. You'll have to keep the **plan on file** at the farm and complete **regular updates**.
- Farmers with a **single tank**, storing **between 5,000 and 10,000 gallons**, cannot use the template, but must instead prepare a **more comprehensive plan** themselves or hire a professional engineer to do it.

Secondary Containment Requirements

Secondary containment is required if you have **more than 1,100 gallons of storage** and this also requires interaction with the state fire marshal to **register** those tanks.

Dikes, containment curbs and pits are common **types** of secondary containment used for this purpose. Diked areas must be sufficiently **impervious** to **contain discharges** and prevent escape of any spilled materials.

The **size** of secondary containment should be adequate to contain the entire capacity of the **largest single container**, with sufficient **freeboard** to contain precipitation. The engineering "rule of thumb" for adequate secondary containment is 110 percent of the largest tank's capacity, plus capacity for a 5.5 inch rain in 24 hours.

Labeling Your Fuel

Essentially, if you have **over 119 gallons** in a fuel tank on a farm service-type truck, you will need a placard identifying what **type of fuel** you are carrying. Diesel and farm gas each have a different **number**. It's not the lottery, so don't just throw some numbers up there. The number on the placard is based on the fuel's **flammability**. Remember to label your off-farm fuel as off-farm. Mixing the red with the non-exempt fuel can lead to big fines against your farm.

7 ESTATE PLANNING

The complex dance of passing the family farm from one generation to the next, while balancing taxation concerns, estate planning, emotional connection to the land, off-farm heirs' expectations, long-term care planning, and lack of family communication, can be overwhelming to almost anyone. Most farm operations have invested dearly in the land, and while others have access to retirement accounts, frequently the land is the only significant source of wealth for the elder generation. If another generation wants to transition the elders out, it becomes difficult.

"Giving up the farm" is more than a transfer of wealth or a dollars-and-cents cash-out. It is a change in lifestyle, status, and profession, a change of identity that affects the sense of heritage and right to control that builds up when one toils through years of blood, sweat, and tears, to create something unique and personal.

Estate Planning Definitions

Knowing these ***basic estate planning definitions*** may be helpful in any conversation you have with an estate planning professional:

- A ***last will and testament*** (usually just called a ***"will"***), is a document that gives your directions on what to do with your property when you die. It takes effect only after you have actually died, and it must be signed by you in the presence of two witnesses. In Iowa, handwritten wills are not recognized as valid.

- A ***trust*** is a legal creature or entity, created by the terms of a document drafted on behalf of a person, the ***grantor*** or ***trustor***, who transfers assets into the trust to be held or used for the benefit of named people (**beneficiaries**). A **trustee**, selected by the grantor, is placed in charge of the trust. Trusts can be used during the grantor's lifetime or contained in a will, to spring to life when the estate is opened. Trusts separate the responsibility of control from the benefit of the income. Trusts can be used when you don't trust someone with asset management but want them to receive the benefit of the asset. They also provide for some "dead hand" control of your assets beyond the grave.

- A **power of attorney** is a document that designates another person who can exercise legal powers for you, during your lifetime - a "pinch hitter," of sorts - if you cannot or choose not to undertake those transactions on your own behalf. A separate document is used for business and medical decisions. Your power of attorney can be revoked by you at any time, and it has no further effect after you die.

Estate Planning is Complex

Many people think that estate planning involves only the creation of a last will and testament, but wills are only one part of a **comprehensive estate plan**. A good estate plan that involves a business will address **tax planning, business succession, financial considerations, off-farm heirs, and the person's individual desires**. These are all fairly heady topics that can't be handled by filling out a standardized form or inputting a little basic information into a do-it-yourself kit. Proper estate planning can often help dramatically **increase the size of the estate that you're able to pass on to your heirs**, while inadequate planning can cause unnecessary losses for your heirs.

Good Estate Planning is a Lifelong Endeavor

Estate planning leads to business planning, which leads to tax planning, which leads to business succession, which should lead to disaster planning, which should lead right back to estate planning. Estate planning can be a bit of a balancing act. In fact, you could look at each estate-planning element as being like a ball in a juggler's performance. At any given moment in time, not every one of the balls can be at the highest point (meaning only one or two of these areas will likely have the benefits currently realized or maximized), and some balls will be on the down-swing (meaning the goal may not be fully implemented, at that time). However, the entire performance only works if each ball is in its appropriate place at the right time.

Your estate planner also needs the experience and skill to identify which balls are glass (meaning they must be handled carefully), which are rubber (which means if they get less priority, they will still likely bounce back into control), and which are lead balls (ones that, if their weight is not properly anticipated, can destroy the entire act).

Good Estate Planning Requires Professional Advice

Historically, farmers have been accused of being nearly religious about not wanting to pay ***income tax***, but simply avoiding income tax may not help you achieve all of your goals Sometimes, depending on the circumstances, paying a little tax now to avoid a big tax later is worth the hit.

> *For example, owning a bunch of machinery that is fully depreciated out to avoid income tax saves an immediate tax, but this method may trigger recapture tax when sold. If an item is sold to a family member, the tax is payable in the first year, even if a contract sale is contemplated for the item. That information may be critical to the 70-year-old mother who is contemplating buying a new tractor with which to feed hay, in a joint operation with her 40-year-old daughter. Effective planning might call for the daughter to buy that piece of equipment, rather than the mother.*

The problem with planning is that it takes time, energy, money, and knowledge about how laws in several areas interplay to produce a final result. You don't learn to juggle these interests overnight. Your estate planning should involve advice from an estate-planning professional. If you hesitate to expend the resources necessary to hire the right act, you can rest assured that your delay will increase the number of lead balls that you'll find yourself juggling, with no prior time to practice.

Consider the following case of family members who did not take the time to plan, or even to communicate with one another, and the disastrous results:

> *A son resigned his non-farm job in 1974 and moved to Wyoming to manage his father's ranch, with the understanding he would inherit the ranch upon the last of his parents to die. In*

1992, the father (the surviving parent) asked the son to leave the ranch. Upon the son's refusal to leave, the father filed an action against the son. The son counterclaimed for breach of contract, alleging that he and his father had an oral contract which provided the son would receive the ranch upon the death of his parents, in exchange for his running the ranch. The trial court determined that an oral contract existed and awarded the land, livestock and machinery to the son, subject to the father's life estate. The father appealed and also amended his estate plan to disinherit the son, making a daughter the sole beneficiary of the father's estate. After the father died, the Wyoming Supreme Court reversed the trial court and said no contract existed. So, the son, after nearly 20 years of work, ended up with no job, no inheritance, strained (at best) family connections, and presumably plenty of legal bills.

If the family above had considered formally and legally structuring the transition from father to son, and had made plans to either include the daughter or provide her with another source of income, the result could have been much different.

While a guide like this one can help equip you with an introduction to some general principles at play in estate planning, it should not substitute for appropriate advice, specific to your situation, from personal consultation with an experienced estate-planning professionals.

Planning

Farm succession planning usually begins when a farm operation is in one of **three stages**:

- A farm that isn't planned to survive past the current generation;
- A farm that is making plans to have the farm survive; or
- A farm that has refused to pick one of the first two.

Oftentimes, certain common, specific **concerns of the elder generation** must be addressed before any plan is approved. These concerns can be wide and varied, but **common succession planning goals of the elder generation** include:

- Preventing a heavy **management burden** upon the surviving spouse;

- Preventing **harm to one's children from** the possible **remarriage** of one's surviving spouse;
- Providing for **off-farm heirs**;
- Retaining **lifetime income flow** for the elder generation; and
- Limiting **estate taxes**.

Succession planning is not something that is usually resolved after Thanksgiving dinner and before the dessert is served. It frequently involves serious discussion and planning by multiple generations of a family.

Competing Interests

The goals and desires of each generation are not often exactly in line with one another. What should be kept mind is that maximization of all aspects of the farm succession plan is highly unlikely. No model has been achieved that simultaneously satisfies all of these **competing interests of multiple generations**:

- An elder generation that wants plenty of income and retained ownership and control of the farm, while not providing labor;
- Off-farm heirs who are entirely satisfied, with no desire to interfere with on-farm heirs' ability to run the farm;
- On-farm heirs who are secure and able to grow the business; and
- Tax-free consequences for everyone involved.

Balancing Goals in Planning

Professionals can provide objective input to a succession plan, to help all of the parties come to a reasonable balance of their objectives and goals. There are usually issues involving the **"golden rule" of estate planning**, which is a little different from the other, more well-known version. In estate planning, **those who have the gold usually make the rules**. While frequently money is the gold, in some family dynamics, labor can be the gold. In any event, it is necessary to have an open and frank discussion regarding who is going to wield the power of **decision-making** and who will receive what benefits.

Business Entities as Planning Tools

With most family farm operations, **business planning** also means estate planning and transition planning. The majority of farm operations are still held by sole proprietorships (meaning no formalized business filing), which means that technically, when the farmer dies, so does the legal existence of the business. This causes upheaval and unnecessary costs to the next generation, if it has any desire to keep farming.

Some multi-generational farms can benefit from more advanced forms of business enterprises, like limited partnerships, limited liability companies and S-Corporations. As discussed in greater detail in the chapter on Planning, each type of business entity offers both advantages and disadvantages, some of which affect estate and succession planning.

C-Corporations ("C-Corps") were once favored by the estate and business-planning community. The advantage to C-Corps include limited liability to share owners, tax deductions not available for other types of entities, and a low tax rate on the first $75,000 of income made. However, the C-Corp has some built-in disadvantages, particularly if it has highly-appreciated land in it.

> *For example, a C corporation owns farmland with a low $1,000 per acre basis. When it goes to sell the ground at $4,000 an acre, not only will it have to pay capital gains tax on the transaction, but when that profit is distributed to the shareholders via dividend, that dividend is subject to tax again. Conversely, if the land had been owned outright by the individuals, only the capital gains tax would be paid.*

Partnerships can happen when two or more people combine resources for a project. Traditionally, the partnership's profits or losses pass through to the partners on either a predetermined percentage or in accordance with their contributions to the partnership. There is no taxation on gain at the partnership level; instead, each individual pays tax on the amount of gain that passes through to him or her individually, avoiding the double taxation of the C-Corp. However, each partner is personally liable for the partnership's debts and each one is fully responsible for the actions of the other partners.

> For example, Joe and Sue begin milking together. Sue orders feed in the partnership name that Joe didn't want delivered. Nevertheless, Joe is just as responsible as Sue for paying the feed bill, and the debt can be collected against Joe's personal assets, like real estate, bank accounts, and other holdings.

A modern business form called a **limited partnership** is a good way to **prevent this unwanted personal liability, while retaining the tax and other advantages of a partnership**. A limited partnership filing allows parties to limit what assets are subject to partnership debts. It also puts creditors on notice that Joe's or Sue's off-farm income from a job may not be available to pay the debts of the partnership.

S-Corporations ("S-Corps") are a meld of partnership principles and the limited liability of corporations. Like partnerships, the S-Corp passes through the losses and gains to the shareholders, so it is **not subject to the double tax problem** that C-Corps face. S-Corps are limited to a certain number of shareholders, and they do not offer all the tax advantages available with a traditional C-Corp.

Limited Liability Companies ("LLCs") are another blend of partnership and corporation principles, and this business form has become a popular alternative to the S-Corp in recent years. LLCs do not have the strict formal requirements of a corporation, which can be burdensome for many business enterprises, but they do provide **liability and asset protection** to the members. For tax purposes, they can be **taxed like a partnership** and pass through the gains and losses, **avoiding double taxation**. If only one person is in the LLC, it can **elect** to be **taxed like a sole proprietorship**, while keeping some liability and contract responsibility protections.

Now, consider just one example demonstrating that a **choice of business form** can be made to produce the greatest advantage, addressing the **competing succession-planning interests** discussed above, when planning a business transition from one generation to the next:

> The elder generation could form an LLC to operate their farm and the LLC could rent the ground from the elders, producing maximum tax advantages and offering limited liability for the LLC's owners. The on-farm heir could work as an employee for the LLC for a short period of time to ensure that operating with the parents is going to work and to acquire the necessary skills

to ensure successful continuation of the business. Then, the on-farm heir can be gifted or buy in to the LLC. Buy-and-sell agreements between the members would outline who could buy out whom, for how much, and when.

Meanwhile, the elders' **estate plan** could provide for the off-farm heirs to receive non-farm assets, while allowing the on-farm heir to inherit the farm. If no off-farm assets exist, valuation mechanisms can be put into place to ensure that the on-farm heir can buy the farm ground from the estate at a reasonable price. This funds the off-farm heirs' estate bequests and prevents the on-farm heir from simply inheriting new landlords (the siblings) when the parents die.

The **elder generation** in this arrangement still **retains an income stream** to provide for its own needs during life, as it sells the membership interest to the next generation and receives rent from the LLC. It has provided itself some **assurance** that the farm's management will be passing into the **competent** hands of the on-farm heir, whose performance has been tested. Finally, it has provided an **inheritance** adequate to satisfy **off-farm heirs' needs**, as well, making it less likely that arguments later among the siblings will lead to legal troubles with the estate, thus ensuring the greatest likelihood of successfully achieving the transfer of the farm operation to the **on-farm heir**.

Property Ownership as a Planning Tool

Who Holds the Cards?

Planning **how a farm holds assets** is as important as acquiring the assets in the first place. When starting any business, an **exit plan** should also be developed. Asset ownership is a component of that plan. Failure to plan can result in unnecessary **exposure of assets to claims of creditors**.

Most farm families purchase **land** jointly between husband and wife. There are different **forms of joint ownership** that they can choose, and the selection of a particular form of joint ownership can affect the issue of who will be in a **decision-making** position, when ownership passes on, after one of them dies. As explained in greater detail in the chapter on Real Estate, joint property ownership between spouses usually takes one of **two common forms**:

- **Joint Tenancy with Rights of Survivorship** - A form of ownership in which each spouse has an **undivided one-half interest** in the entire property (The property is not physically divided in half). When the first **"joint tenant"** dies, the survivor takes title to the entire property through **operation of the law** of property ownership, with **no need for probate** (i.e., ownership rights need not pass through a probate estate action).

- **Tenancy in Common** – Another form of ownership, in which the two parties again own an **undivided one-half interest** in the property, but when one of the **"tenants in common"** dies, that person's **half interest passes via probate** (with or without a will) to the dead tenant's **heirs**. This allows for a "step up" in the tax basis of the property for capital gains purposes, and can be used to bring in the next generation as a co-owner with the surviving spouse.

A **"step up in basis"** is a tax concept that allows a person who receives property from an estate to only pay **capital gains tax** on the **difference between date of death value and the date of sale**. If the property is gifted to the person while the donor is alive, the cost that the donor paid for the property **transfers** to the new person and becomes that person's tax basis, with resulting higher capital gains tax to be paid if the property is eventually sold.

> Consider the difference in capital gains tax between a farm bought in 1950 for $300 an acre and given to the next generation during the owner's lifetime. If the next generation turned around to sell it at market price in 2011 at $10,000 per acre, capital gains would be paid on $9,700 per acre. Conversely, if the next generation inherited the property in 2011, and sold it for $12,000 an acre in 2014, only $2,000 per acre would be subject to capital gain tax.

On occasion, the elder generation has one farm-operating spouse and one non-operating spouse. Historically, the male has been the farm operator, and males, on average, die first. Depending on how things are set up, death of the operating spouse could leave the non-operating spouse in a sudden position of total ownership. Having both spouses involved in the process of estate planning and business transition is important, both to the spouses and to those in the next generation, who expect a certain outcome. Promises made by a dead parent are rarely enforceable against another parent who decides not to honor them, unless some prior action is taken, to set up legal rights that will fulfill those promises.

Transfer of Power

Next, the concept of **power transfer** needs to be addressed. Some elderly landowners believe that, unless they hold the ground, the younger generation will ignore them, fail to take care of them, or place them in managed care, never to see the light of day again. Addressing this concern is an important facet of transition planning.

A method that works with some success is the **transfer with lease-back**, which means that the elder generation transfers the land to the next generation, but retains a lease back to the elder generation for a reasonable number of years.

> **Note:** If done at least **five years** prior to requiring Medicare support for nursing home care, this can be an effective way to **avoid probate** and avoid exposing an asset to recovery by the **Iowa's Estate Recovery Team**.

The lease provides some security for the elder generation and allows them to be on the farm for as long as they like. The down side is that, unless the land is already paid for, it is a hard thing to acquire an asset and then lease it back to the elder generation, if a mortgage has to be paid from the asset. In addition, with a transfer like this, the next generation misses out on the step-up in tax basis, opening up the possibility of higher capital gains taxes down the road.

For many years, a **life estate to the surviving spouse with a remainder interest to the children** was a cheap, effective way to pass real estate without a lot of complex will-drafting. Further, it ensured that a second spouse and that spouse's children didn't "get their hands on" family assets, usually farm ground. The elder generation essentially got to behave as if the ground was still entirely theirs (rent collected, taxes paid, military and homestead exemptions applied) until their death.

Property is like a bundle of sticks. Each aspect of property (right to use, responsibility to pay taxes, mineral rights, wind farm rights) is one of the sticks in the bundle. Under a life estate, one person (the **life estate holder),** holds onto the right to occupy and use the property, along with the responsibility to pay the taxes. Another person or people (the **remaindermen**) hold the rest, and when the life estate holder dies, all of those "sticks" transfer to the remaindermen.

Modern legal realities have weakened the value of the life estate as an estate-planning tool. First, while the transfer of full ownership occurs upon the life estate holder's death, the remainderman cannot take those sticks without clearing a **Medicaid lien** on the property. The value of the life estate holder's interest is figured just prior to his death. This can mean that, despite transfer of substantial interest in the farm prior to death, a life estate holder on Title 19 assistance can be made to pay back part of money advanced for their care in a long-term care facility.

Second, the **tax basis** for a life estate property is established at the **time of creation of the life estate**, not at death. If it was not a sale with a retained life estate, then the remaindermen get the transferor's presumably low basis in the property, **not the higher "stepped up" basis** that they would have received had the property been transferred via **probate** proceedings.

Matters become even more tangled and snarled when folks create life estates that span multiple generations, restraining the future ability of interested parties to sell the property. For example, a person might retain a life estate to their spouse, then a life estate to their children, and then make the grandchildren the remaindermen. This can **run afoul of federal gift tax law** because the gift to the grandchildren is a gift of a **future interest**, and no gift tax exclusion is available for such a gift.

While the life estate may still have some applicability In estate planning, its use as a quick and easy way to altogether avoid the need for real succession planning should be fading.

Gifts as Planning Tools

An individual can give **up to $5 million during his or her lifetime without paying a gift tax**, and for **couples** that threshold is **$10 million**. As land prices continue to rise, a smart estate plan could utilize the gift tax exclusion to pass on highly-valued farm ground to the next generation. If a gift recipient decides to sell, the land's presumably **low basis also transfers** with the title, creating a capital gains tax issue.

The higher gift tax exemption is only on the books until 2013, so those who take a long time to contemplate it may be left out in the dust.

The capital gains event can be wiped out by holding on to the property until death. However, the land is then subject to creditors' claims, and if the value rises, the estate is put in the position of having to pay estate tax, which is usually higher than capital gains tax .

Deciding the best course of action requires a delicate balancing of interests, and no single course of action fits all parties. The question is what the next generation intends to do with the property that it is slated to receive. The best answer may determine when and how the next generation receives it.

Selling to your family members

Here's one final word on planning, as it affects deals you make with family members. Family members get sweetheart deals on real estate and equipment all the time. Be warned, though - If you sweeten the pot too much, the IRS will throw some vinegar in the mix in the name of fairness.

*Consider, for example, selling your line of machinery to your daughter as she grows her farm operation. If you sell her the tractor one year and the haybine the next, that is not a problem. However, if you sell her the entire line over a period of years, the IRS will invoke the **"related party rule"** and demand payment in the first year of the contract, as if the seller received all the proceeds from the contract sale in year one.*

8 GETTING PAID

Getting paid for what you do is obviously a business necessity, without which your operations will not continue to function for long. Fortunately, certain legal mechanisms called **agricultural liens** are available to make it easier to ensure that you do, in fact, get paid at the end of the day.

An **agricultural lien** is an **encumbrance**, filed against **farm products or property**, to **secure payment for services and goods** provided to a farm operation or rent on farm property. Liens can operate for you, or those who provide services and goods to your operation can file liens against your property, so it is good to be familiar with the situations that give rise to various liens related to your farm operations.

Iowa has **Landlord's Liens, Ag Supplier's Liens, Harvester's Liens, Custom Cattle Feeding Liens, Commodity Production Liens, Service Animal Liens, and Veterinarian's Liens.** The names of these liens give a good indication of the type of service or goods that each one provides coverage for.

On the other hand, some Iowa liens that could affect you bear names that can be a little misleading or aren't really ag liens, in the strictest sense of the word. Two liens that are not technically ag liens (because they require you to hold the goods) are **Artisan's Liens** and **Care of Stock Liens**. These two liens do not take **priority** over (or jump in front of) other, competing liens held against the same property. An Artisan's lien is not for artists, but rather for mechanics, who provide improvements to equipment through repair and modification (Ironically titled, a "**Mechanic's Lien**" does exist, but it protects those who improve real property!)

Always Check the Rules on Liens

Each one of the liens available under Iowa law has specific rules for the **proper form for the lien papers**, **when to file it** and **what priority the lien is given** when competing against other liens. The chart on the following page helps summarize it, but failure to follow the current law can leave you holding an empty bag.

Lien	Who files	Against What	Does filer have to hold the property	When to file
Landlord	Property owner	Tenants crops	No	Within 20 days of tenant's possession
Ag Supplier	Retail sellers of ag supplies	Crops and livestock produced by the supplied items	No	When credit is granted
Harvester	Custom harvest operator	Crop harvested	No	Within 10 days after harvest
Artisan	Repairer or improver of personal property	The property improved	YES, hold the property to keep perfection	NA
Care of Stock	Stable keepers, herders,	Property kept	Yes	NA
Service Animals	Owners of stallion, jack or bull or AI company	Serviced animals' offspring	No	Filed with the sheriff's office to seize the offspring and sell them

Veterinarian	Veterinarian	Livestock treated or provided service by vet	No	Within 60 days of service
Mechanic's	Person who furnishes material, labor or services to real property	The real property improved	No	Filed with Clerk of Court
Cattle Feeder	Feed lot operator	Cattle and cash proceeds	No	Within 20 days of cattle arriving
Commodity Contractor	Producer in a contract to produce good	Livestock, milk, crops produced or proceeds	No	45 days after planting or arrival of livestock

9 COMMODITY SALES

Commodity sales are a central core component of many farm operations. The operator, of course, can ***sell on the market upon delivery***, take a ***price-later contract***, sell on a ***deferred payment contract***, or ***store*** the commodity.

The old joke is that farmers only sell $5.00 they are waiting for it to go to $10.50.

The general concept is to use the market to remove risk that the production of the product creates. Not all marketers are created equal and if you don't enjoy following market trends, the weather in South America, and the Chinese government's latest import policy, you can hire professional advisors. Many ag industry companies offer market updates via cell phone text messages sent multiple times day or offer pay-for-advice text messages to help people follow market trends.

Marketing is hard and if you let your emotions or your desire to brag at the coffee shop interfere, it can make a tough job even tougher. One technique is to figure your cost of production and expected return at a reasonable price per unit sold. Then determine what you would do with that return, for example, purchase a new grain bin. Get a picture of that grain bin and the minute you don't sell at the price that would allow that return, tear up the picture, as that is what you are giving up.

Grain Storage

When storing grain in a licensed public facility, certain rules and protections exist for the farm operator. In such storage arrangements, a ***warehouse receipt*** stating the number of bushels deposited is usually issued. The warehouse receipt stands as evidence of ownership of the grain. The warehouse receipt is issued usually at the close of delivery of the product.

Whenever the grain is moved in or out, a **scale house ticket** is issued. This is the document issued to the driver who delivers. This is not quite the same a warehouse receipt, as most facilities allow a short time to decide what to do (open time) with the product.

Common Sale Contracts

Cash-forward contracts are agreements that set a price for actual delivery of a commodity at a future date. This is a method used by both purchasers and sellers, to ensure a set price for set bushels or head, and it is a great tool to cover the costs of production for operators.

Price-later contracts also involve delivery of a set amount on a set date, but unlike cash-forward contracts, the price is set and paid later. Some pricing methods allow for setting a specific future date and time, when the price for the product will be determined. Others allow a discount (basis) from a set date, as selected later by the farmer.

Deferred payment agreements envision a current sale, delivery, and price-setting, with payment withheld until a specified later date. This arrangement is commonly used for end-of-year **tax planning**. The farmer must have no ability to demand the payment earlier, if he hopes to convince the IRS the payment was not available at the time of sale. The Packers and Stockyard Act requires settlement of livestock sales within 72 hours of delivery, so using this arrangement with livestock sales has risk.

Minimum-price contracts set a floor for price but also allow a chance to participate in upswings in the market. Examine these contracts carefully, as they are not offered by the commodity merchant without **built-in pricing protections** in favor of the merchant, as well.

Futures Contracts

Futures contracts are standard agreements set by a **commodity exchange** for a predefined quantity of a commodity. A seller and a buyer each promise to fill in the details of when it will be delivered and what price will be paid. A **seller is "going long,"** while a **buyer is "going short."**

The futures contract doesn't mean that you have the product at the time when the contract is made, but it indicates you **will** have it to deliver at a later date. Most futures contracts are **reversed** or **liquidated** before the delivery date occurs, though there are some great stories of inattentive traders being delivered 5,000 lbs. of beef or 50,000 lbs. of cotton float through the traders' tales. That is because some buyers, like processors, actually want the product, and the seller runs the risk of not being able to offset the delivery with another purchase.

Hedging

Hedging is a futures-trading method of **managing risk**. To have a true hedge, you take a position opposite to your current position. Typical hedgers also include speculators, who believe they will purchase low and sell high and sell low and buy high. Grain dealers typically take the hedge risk, but in today's sophisticated market, farm operators are tempted to become directly involved. Detailed study should be undertaken before diving into the hedge market.

A **hedge-to-arrive ("HTA") contract** is a contract used in futures trading in which the futures price is determined when the contract is created, but the basis level is not determined until later, usually just before delivery. A **standard HTA** contract is a **forward contract** in which the farmer promises to deliver a stated quantity of grain for a **price linked to the price of a futures contract that expires in the delivery month**.

- From the **farmer's perspective**, such an HTA contract is a normal forward contract that shifts to the buyer the risk that the market price will fall before delivery (and simultaneously prevents the farmer from taking advantage of rising prices).
- From the **buyer's perspective**, the HTA contract facilitates hedging.

Failure to Deliver

A **failure to deliver** according to the required terms of any of these contracts can be treated by the other party as a **breach of contract,** unless it is **excused.** An event not related to the farmer's control may be an **excuse or justification** for failure to deliver, if the contract is based upon a **specific parcel**. However, events like this will **not** excuse performance on contracts which are merely based on **commodities of a certain type and kind**.

Put another way, consider this: One valid excuse for failure to perform any contract is **impossibility** of performance. Impossibility can result from different kinds of unexpected causes, like **natural disasters,** to name just one. However, when it comes to delivering commodities, your performance of the obligation to deliver may only be made impossible, if your contract required you to deliver something like commodities from a specific parcel, which cannot be replaced by commodities grown just anywhere.

> *For example, as a farm operator, if you have a contract to deliver seed beans grown on certain named farmland, and a tornado comes along and destroys them, it has become impossible to comply with the very clear terms of the contract. Because the beans you agreed to deliver were only those grown on a specific parcel, you are likely excused from your obligation to deliver.*

On the other hand, even unexpected events will **not** excuse your performance, if the product you have agreed to deliver is replaceable.

> *For example, if you have a contract to deliver 5,000 bushels of beans to the elevator, and you planned to fulfill that obligation by delivering beans from your farm, but the crop protection company sprays your beans with the wrong chemical, killing off the crop, you are still on the hook to deliver beans, from wherever you can get them.*

In such a scenario, though, you may be able to recover your damages from the crop protection company (or its insurance company), by filing a claim against it for negligence.

There are other legal defenses, such as **mutual mistake** or **incapacity**, which apply to excuse performance of commodities contracts. Consider this example:

> *A great story floats around about the farmer who "locked in" corn at $4.00 a bushel. When the price shot up to $7.00 a bushel, the tale goes that he had himself checked into a mental facility and declared incompetent, in order to void the contracts. To even the casual observer, his sudden motivation*

for "seeking help" was clearly a ruse, to allow him a chance to take advantage of the higher prices. Nevertheless, it worked.

Although the story above may seem to be an extreme example, the fact is that ***incapacity to form a contract***, declared by qualified doctors, provided that fellow with a ***valid excuse*** not to perform the contract, at all. See the chapter on Contracts, for more details about situations that could excuse performance.

10 GRAIN INDEMNITY AND DEALER LICENSING

The **Iowa Grain Indemnity Fund** can provide some protection to farmers who experience certain **losses** on grain stored in a **state-licensed warehouse** or sold to a **state-licensed grain dealer**.

All grain producers pay into the Iowa Grain Indemnity Fund. The **Iowa Department of Agriculture and Land Stewardship (IDALS)** administers the Grain Indemnity Fund, which acts as a form of self –insurance for producers, to provide partial reimbursement of losses from selling grain or storing grain with an elevator that fails. IDALS also administers Iowa's licensing programs for grain dealers and warehouses.

What Is Covered

Limits on Indemnity: How Much can you Get Back?

The Iowa Grain Indemnity Fund provides a guarantee of **some, limited recovery.** The Fund works in a way similar to the FDIC bank deposit guarantee, in that it won't give you back the full amount of what you've lost; limits are imposed on how much a grain producer can claim against the fund.

The Fund pays the claimant producer for **90 percent of loss, up to a maximum of $300,000.00 per claimant**. That's 30,000 bushels of $10.00 beans.

The value of your claim is determined by the status of your relationship with the dealer that just failed. If you have a check, you have a different relationship with the dealer than if you have grain in the facility.

You will be able to make a claim against the Fund and also against the individual dealer, who may have the actual grain seized and administered under a limited receivership by the State.

Grain Sold to a Licensed Dealer

Coverage on **grain sold** to a licensed grain dealer is **limited** to **sales** that took place **within six months of the date when the government revokes the dealer's license or when the dealer declares bankruptcy by filing in federal court.** For sold grain, the coverage is typically provided on **priced grain** delivered to a dealer that has not yet been paid for but that is **not considered a credit sale contract**; and on **grain checks** that have been returned for insufficient funds from the grain dealer's bank and are **not more than six months old**. If you are concerned about a bounced check from the grain dealer, take action to collect it immediately. Don't rest on a dealer's oral assurances that everything will be okay.

Grain Stored in a Licensed Warehouse

For **stored grain**, there is no distinction made between grain on warehouse receipts and grain that is in "open storage" or "unsettled."

- Grain that is **priced at the time of delivery** is not stored; it is sold and the **coverage is provided**.
- **Unpriced grain on a credit-sale** contract is not stored; it is sold and **no coverage is provided**.

The rule of thumb is that if you are still "playing the board," or waiting on a better price, you are exposed to risk and you may find that you have no recovery in the event of a grain dealer's collapse.

What Is Not Covered

USDA-Licensed Warehouses

The Iowa Grain Indemnity Fund does not provide coverage of grain stored in a warehouse licensed by USDA. In that case, you would seek repayment directly from the USDA, which requires its warehouse operators to be **bonded**, under the terms of their federal warehouse operator licenses.

No Coverage for Credit Sale Contracts

A **credit-sale contract** is a contract for the **sale of grain** pursuant to which the **sale price is to be paid more than 30 days after the grain is delivered to the buyer**. Credit-sale contracts include those contracts commonly referred to as **deferred payment, deferred pricing, price-later, basis** and **minimum-price contracts**.

The Iowa Grain Indemnity Fund provides **no coverage for losses in a credit-sale contract situation**. This is an important point to note, because grain producers sometimes decide to defer receiving payment as a **tax-planning technique**. However, given the volatile status of today's market, these producers risk total loss, if the grain dealer or warehouse fails.

In such an arrangement, the grain producer essentially serves as a banker to the elevator, by allowing delayed payment. Most bankers require financial statements in advance of lending money, and they protect their interests with security agreements or mortgages. Yet, producers who defer grain payments may not ask for those types of documents or take other steps necessary to secure their position in such a transaction.

> *Although credit-sale contracts are risky business of the kind that is generally not advisable, if you do plan to use credit-sale contracts as a form of tax planning, do so only with competent legal advice.*

If done correctly, proper security documents can give you a **security interest** in **specific assets** of the grain dealer to collect against and **priority**, or first rights, when it comes to collecting. Without security, if your grain dealer goes under before you get paid, you will be left in the lurch, forced to sue for what you can get (if there's anything left to get), and you'll have no protection from the Iowa Grain Indemnity Fund. Unfortunately, most large grain dealers are not going to provide you with proper security, so you need to keep your eyes open in advance of deferring that payment.

Dealer-to-Dealer Sales

No coverage is provided on grain sold by one grain dealer to another. Take note, that even if you're not a licensed grain dealer, certain actions you take can cause the state to treat you like a grain dealer.

> *For example, with greater market volatility and greater storage capacity at home, you may be tempted to buy grain from your neighbor directly. In some cases, this could cause you to be classified as a grain dealer.*

A "**producer**" is defined in the law to be the **owner, tenant, or operator of land** in Iowa who has an **interest in grain produced** on that land. On the other hand, an **Iowa grain dealer license** is required of most persons who purchase more than *1,000 bushels of grain from producers in any month, for delivery in Iowa*. There are exceptions to this general rule (*see Grain Dealer Licensing*, below).

Grain Dealer Licensing

Because the Grain Indemnity Fund only protects producers who have sold to an IDALS-licensed grain dealer, it is important to know a few things about grain dealer licensing. Additionally, in case you are kicking around getting into the business of purchasing and selling grain, consider the obligations carefully. As a general rule, any person who purchases *1,000 bushels of grain or more from producers during any month, if such grain is delivered in the state of Iowa*, must be **licensed** by IDALS as a *grain dealer*.

Iowa Code Section 203.1(10) lists the entire set of **exceptions to the grain dealer licensing requirements**, which include:

- A person who buys **fewer than 1,000 bushels per month**;
- A person who is a **producer who buys grain for his or her own use** as seed or feed;
- And other ag industry players with specific exemptions.

Classes of IDALS Grain Dealer Licenses

There are two **classes of grain dealer licenses**:

- A **class one** license has **no limit** on the amount of purchases, and an authorized class one dealer **may be allowed to purchase grain by credit-sale contracts**.

- A ***class two*** license-holder may not purchase more than **$500,000** from producers per fiscal year. ***NO grain purchases by credit-sale contract*** are allowed, in any amount.

  NOTE: As mentioned earlier, a **credit-sale contract** is any contract for the sale of grain pursuant to which the sale price is to be paid **more than 30 days after delivery** of the grain to the buyer, including contracts like those usually called deferred payment, deferred pricing, price-later, basis and minimum-price contracts.

Class one grain dealers may issue credit-sale contracts only if they are authorized. To be authorized, the grain dealer must either file a ***bond*** or ***letter of credit*** in the amount of ***$100,000*** or file an ***audited financial statement***.

Net Worth, Current Ratio, and Financial Statement Filings

Class one grain dealers must ***maintain*** a ***net worth*** of ***$75,000***. ***Class two grain dealers*** must maintain a net worth of ***$37,500***. ***All grain dealers must maintain a current ratio of 1:1.*** This means that for every dollar of current liabilities you have, you must have at least one dollar of current assets. To ***issue credit-sale contracts***, grain dealers must have a ***minimum net worth equal to 50 cents per bushel*** of grain carried on credit-sale contract.

After the initial licensing application, ***grain dealers must file a financial statement*** within three months of the end of their fiscal year. Fiscal year-end financial statements must include a balance sheet, income statement, statement of cash flows and the notes to the financial statements.

Sole proprietor grain dealers must file a ***personal financial statement*** in addition to the ***business financial statement*** on the sole proprietorship. The balance sheet for the personal financial statement must show the assets both at their historical cost basis (original cost, less depreciation) and at their fair-market value.

All financial statements that are filed must be either ***audited*** or reviewed by an Iowa Certified Public Accountant (CPA), The financial statements must be prepared in accordance with generally accepted accounting principles.

NOTE: *Grain dealers are required to maintain the minimum net worth and current ratio at all times, not just when the financial statements are filed!*

Mandatory Record-Keeping

Grain dealers are required to keep complete and accurate ***records of all grain purchased***. Dealers must maintain a ***daily position record for each type of grain***, which shows the increase, decrease and ending balance, including grain that the dealer has purchased, but not made payment for. Dealers must also utilize ***pre-numbered settlement sheets*** and ***pre-numbered credit-sale contracts***.

- All ***scale tickets*** must be filed in a ***daily order***;
- Settlement sheets must be filed alphabetically; and
- Contracts must be filed numerically.

Grain dealers are subject to ***inspection*** by the department during the hours of 8 a.m. to 5 p.m., Monday through Friday. Dealers are required to have an office or business location ***open*** during these hours.

Interestingly enough, if a third party buys grain from a grain dealer, then even though records can clearly trace the transactions back to a warehouse receipt of the farmer who put the grain in storage, the storing farmer will still lose to the third-party purchaser.

11 INSURANCE

Insurance is all around us. Every day, we use a variety of insurance policies, like health insurance, life insurance, property insurance, liability insurance, motor vehicle insurance, or even vacation insurance, to manage risks we face.

An insurance policy is a contract, drafted by a team of lawyers and reviewed by an army of risk-analysis specialists and accountants, all employed by the insurance company, all working with an eye toward profit. The last thing an insurance contract is designed to do is protect you, unless you behave in a certain manner, as very specifically defined by the wording of the insurance policy. Insurance companies all claim to be superior guardians of your interests, but when it comes down to it, insurance companies only do three things very well: **Deny** claims, **delay** claims, and **defend** claims.

Your full disclosure of every conceivable detail is usually required of you by the terms of an insurance policy. For example, you might have spent a good deal of money buying fire insurance to cover your outbuildings, but unless you told your insurance company beforehand that your wood shack contains open-flame roasting pits, you will very likely find coverage denied, if the shack goes up in smoke or your buddy receives personal injuries from cooking in there.

"Liability"

With insurance, it is important to understand the concept of **liability**. Liability means **responsibility**.

Liability can be based on **intentional, voluntary actions** (like assaulting someone, as by punching them). Liability can also arise over things one might consider "accidents," where there is **negligence** (the failure to take reasonable steps to avoid causing harm that you could have foreseen, like failing to keep a good eye on a burning field and "accidentally" burning down your neighbor's barn). Finally, you can face **strict liability** for harm that is caused by your failure to follow the law - even where the resulting harm is likely not what the law was intended to prevent.

> *For example, say you have a completely toothless and harmless old pet tiger. The law says that all captive tigers must be caged, and such a law is obviously intended to prevent harm your tiger couldn't inflict, like casualties to your neighbor's livestock (or personal injury to your neighbor, for that matter). Nevertheless, if you violate the law by allowing your tiger to roam free, and its nap on your neighbor's car roof leaves a deep dent, you'll be held **strictly liable** for the cost of repairs.*

Picking the Right Insurance Policy

Knowing the lay of the land of insurance is important to farm operators, big and small. You might be tempted to save money on **insurance premiums** (the cost of the insurance) by hand-selecting only **limited coverages** that you think you are likely to need, by selecting **high deductibles** (the out-of-pocket amount you're responsible for, if a loss occurs) or simply by purchasing **inadequate amounts** of insurance that won't pay out what you will need to stay up and running, if a loss occurs.

While a standard **farmowners insurance policy** and **motor vehicle insurance** may wind up covering most of the loss or liability issues you might reasonably expect to face, you should never believe for a minute that the world might not offer you up one of its truly bizarre accidents. These things all happen to someone, normally a person who wasn't expecting it, and they very well could happen to you.

When it comes to insuring your farm operations, your best bet is to get an **umbrella policy,** a special additional coverage for liability not covered by your regular farmowners insurance and motor vehicle coverage, with a **large coverage** amount. An umbrella policy is like life insurance for your operation. When something bad happens, it is a good source of funds, and funds make most business problems go away.

Exclusions from Coverage

An insurance contract usually carves out **exclusions from coverage.** Exclusions are losses that the insurance policy simply will not cover.

Most policies do not cover losses that result from **intentional acts**, like theft by employees over a certain amount, assaults, or alcohol-related events. Other exclusions may relate more specifically to the type of insurance involved. For example, a typical farmowners policy might not be adequate to insure against losses suffered from the flooding of a nearby creek.

Read through your insurance policy carefully, **before** you pay the premium, and when in doubt, ask your agent to point out language that provides the coverage you need. No matter what an agent tells you that you're buying, when a loss occurs, you are going to be stuck with whatever coverage is provided by the language in your written insurance policy. If you wait until a loss has occurred before you take the first deep look at your policy, you may be surprised to find that coverage for your loss is excluded.

Some insurance contracts can be confusing. It is not unusual for insurance companies to issue **standard-form policy** documents that appear to include common exclusions from coverage, accompanied by "**riders**," which are additional pages that are attached to the policies and may actually provide for a coverage excluded in the main document. These riders are part of your policy, and the entire policy, with riders, should be kept in a safe location.

Coverage of Property Damage or Losses

Types of Coverage

Know the type of coverage you are getting. For example **basic coverage**, **broad form coverage**, and **special coverage** on farm buildings are each designed to cover different kinds of losses.

Basic coverage is intended to compensate you for losses from causes like fire, lightning, explosion, windstorm, hail, riot or civil commotion, aircraft or vehicle, vandalism, theft, sinkhole collapse, and volcanic action (Hopefully, you won't have to worry about the last one in Iowa!). Broad form coverage would include all of the above and add additional coverage for damage from causes like the weight of ice, snow, or sleet; falling objects; and accidental discharges of water. Purchasing special coverage would get you the protection included in the basic and broad coverage, but special coverage also offers what is called **open peril coverage**, in which other causes of damage are covered, unless they are **specifically excluded** under the farm policy (like, for example, a flood loss).

Documenting Property Losses, Before they Occur

Documenting details is important, when it comes to making claims against an insurance policy, and many insurance contracts require it. Even if you experience damage that would clearly have been covered by your insurance policy, you may be out of luck if you haven't specifically documented the **existence and value of an asset** to the company and you have nothing to prove what you've lost. In fact, not only could your insurance claim be denied, but you could also lose other benefits, like **casualty loss tax deductions** on your income-tax returns.

> For example, a homeowner was denied a casualty loss deduction by the IRS because, while the homeowner had pictures of a fire that destroyed his home, the homeowner had no pictures of the items he claimed to have lost in the fire. This prevented determining the value of the items.

A simple way to avoid this problem is to take a **pre-loss inventory** of your items, using free **inventory forms** available online from providers like www.knowyourstuff.org. You can upload **pictures**, assign what **room** the item is in, and add items like **serial numbers** and **purchase prices**. All of this information is **stored** online, plus you can **print** the document and **file** it with your insurance agency. As one local agent suggests, no adjuster is going to pay for 20 leisure suits based solely on your word, but a picture of 20 leisure suits is hard to argue against.

If nothing else, take a few minutes and **use your smart phone to photograph** your shop tools, manuals and other things. Many of your smaller things that you are not likely to remember in the event of a large loss are still expensive to replace. Use the phone to take a photo of the data plate with the serial number of your equipment, large and small. Then transfer them to a memory stick and throw it in your personal safe.

> *For example, think about how many expensive electronic gadgets your family may have that, if trashed by rain following a roof collapse, would "have to" be replaced. Consider whether those gadgets should be listed with your insurance company.*

Your agent should be kept up to date on your **new purchases**, as well. If you added a John Deere 4440 to the farm inventory, but never declared it to the company, it is a lot harder to make a claim, when a tree falls on it or it is stolen. Your agent can help you by binding the company when you acquire new property, but you should report it quickly, because many policies allow you just 30 days to get property listed on your policy after it is acquired.

Liability Insurance

Liability insurance protects you, when you have liability for **damage to other people or their property**. Your liability coverage may protect you if the damage was caused by your **negligence** or by some activity for which you have **strict liability**. Liability insurance policies usually have specific coverage **exclusions** for damages you cause **intentionally**.

Most farmers use a **Farmers Comprehensive Personal Liability policy (FCPL)**. Some of the basics of this policy generally include:

- **Bodily injury** at a set amount of coverage, which varies by policy;
- **Property damage** at a set amount, which varies by policy.
- A **duty to defend** the policyholder, which is carried out by hiring an attorney chosen by the company and controlling that attorney's right to settle. What this means is that, even if you are dead-set against settling, the company has the right to do so. In addition, once the company pays out its policy limits, it has no further duty to defend you. Look to see if the cost of defense comes out of the policy limits or is a separate item.
- **Exclusions**. What you see in big print is often modified, updated, and changed in the fine print. Many times, family

members and the policyholders cannot receive payments for injuries they sustain. Pollution claims (including harm caused by chemical release from hog confinements) and business activities other than farming (selling soap, lemonade stands, quilt shops, etc.) may be excluded unless specifically mentioned as covered activities.

Custom farm work may require an additional "rider" to the policy to cover your actions, or a policy may provide coverage only as long as you don't exceed a certain amount of custom work (for example $1,000). **Horses** may or may not be covered. Check the print. Providing lessons to the neighbor kid one time is a lot different than operating a weekly school. The insurance company has the right to know what risks it is insuring against and to charge higher premiums, accordingly. In addition, **ATVs** may or may not be covered under a farm policy. Ask questions and get the answers **before** someone is hurt.

Documenting Accidents and Damages

If you're in an accident or if someone else notifies you that they intend to make a claim against your insurance, you should take time as soon as possible to **make written notes** of every detail you can remember, including anything said by the other people involved. If it is at all possible, **take photographs** with your smart phone.

> For example, photos taken at an **accident scene**, including both close-ups of **damage**, as well as distance photos showing the relative **positions of vehicles** and any other relevant factors, can make all the difference in the world, when an insurance claim is made or a lawsuit is filed against you. Sometimes, photographing **property damage** can prevent a claimant from later claiming that there was more damage than there really was or from inflating the value of the thing damaged.

Borrowing and Lending Equipment

If you let your neighbor use your semi tractor and trailer, and he gets in an accident while using them,, your insurance (not your neighbor's) is going to pay the claim. The only way to shift this responsibility is to insist on having a written rental agreement that clearly assigns the responsibility to the neighbor leasing your equipment. Although many neighbors may want to "make it right," seeing the high estimated cost of repair often dampens that initial offer.

Keeping Insurance Information Handy

As one final bit of advice, consider taking a picture of your policy declaration page and insurance agent's telephone number with your smart phone. Leave it on there. If you have an accident on the road with a tractor, you may not have insurance cards or a glove box to put them in. Also, if one of your employees gets in an accident, it is an easy way to get the information to the investigating officer quickly.

12 LABOR AND THE LAW

Most farm operations employ labor of one sort or another, but hiring others to work on your farm opens the operation to regulation from state and federal agencies that administer **labor laws.** This chapter discusses who qualifies as an "employee" (as opposed to an "independent contractor") and points out some basic steps you should take for employees, such as getting your workman's compensation insurance coverage in place, obtaining a **federal tax identification number**, and putting together the documents and information you need to conduct **tax withholding**.

Employee vs. Independent Contractor

The distinction between **employee** and **independent contractor** is crucial in just about every area of law that affects the labor you hire to work on your farm operation (or elsewhere). As a general rule, **employees receive more benefits or protection from these laws** than do independent contractors. Employers who classify workers as independent contractors do not have to withhold federal and state income taxes for employees, nor do the employers have to pay Social Security taxes, carry workman's' compensation insurance, or pay unemployment taxes for these workers.

It shouldn't be too surprising, then, that in most of these situations, the people you hire to work for you are first **assumed to be employees**; if you want to prove that your labor is not entitled to various labor law advantages (all of which generally require either more money or more work, or both, from the employer), it is usually **your burden to prove** that the person you hired was an **independent contractor**.

In general, the question of "employee vs. independent contractor" is one of **control over the details of the work:**

- If the **operator controls how, when and where** the other party works, it looks a lot like an **employer-employee relationship**.
- If the person you've hired sets his or her own **hours**, provides his or her own **equipment**, and does **similar work for other operators**, it begins to look more like an **independent contractor relationship**.

It is important to realize, too, that the labels you put on your relationship with your workers do not control their legal classification.

> For example, consider the difference between a neighbor who combines for hire after his own fields are harvested, using his own combine; and a retired farmer, who combines for just one active farmer, takes orders from the active farmer about when and where to combine, and uses the active farmer's combine. No matter what you call these relationships, the government is more than likely going to find that the first is an independent contractor, and the second is an employee.

Workman's Compensation

Before a farm operation pays someone to do something as an employee, **workman's compensation insurance ("workman's comp")** needs to be secured. Designed to protect workers injured on the job, this insurance provides **automatic benefits and medical coverage** to **employees** who are **injured** while working **"in the course and scope of employment,"** including benefits for treatment of the injury, temporary or healing period benefits, and permanent disability benefits.

Workman's comp represents a compromise. In return for the certainty of receiving automatic benefits for work-related injuries, a covered employee accepts the **limited remedy** of receiving **only the benefits** provided under the workman's comp law; he or she **cannot sue the employer** for negligence to recover traditional court-awarded damages.

Workman's compensation insurance to cover employees is required by law, but it is secured by you, through a private insurance agent. While it is **not** necessary to cover true **independent contractors** with workman's comp, you'd better be able to prove that someone injured while working on your farm was not actually an employee. If you don't obtain coverage, there are consequences:

- First, there's **no "limited remedy" protection** for an employer who isn't carrying workman's comp insurance. You can be held personally liable for the employee's injuries, meaning that the **employee can sue you and can collect any judgment against your assets**. If an injury occurred while the employee was working for you, **you are presumed to be liable** for the injuries. The burden of proof will be upon you as the employer to prove that you aren't liable. This burden of proof is significant, because it is a complete reversal from the usual injury lawsuit, which normally requires the injured person to prove that a defendant was at fault for causing his injuries.
- In addition, you could face **criminal liability** for failing to obtain workman's compensation insurance when you should.

While the owner of a company can **exempt** himself or herself from the obligation to carry workman's comp insurance coverage, by applying to the Iowa Insurance Commissioner to become "**self-insured**," a decision to go this way is often pennywise and pound-foolish. As farming is consistently listed as one of the most dangerous occupations, it would be wise to consult your agent before waiving this potential source of income protection.

> For example, consider the possibilities, if a hired worker lost an arm or a leg in a combine accident. Workman's compensation insurance would cover and provide medical treatment and perhaps a lump-sum benefit to an injured employee. A court, on the other hand, could award a person with such injuries millions of dollars in damages for current and future medical expenses, pain and suffering, loss of the ability to have a normal relationship with a spouse, or even punitive damages, all of which could be collected against anything and everything you own.

A **workman's compensation claim** is handled under its own set of laws, requires the company to investigate, and has relaxed evidence rules. An injured employee who feels that he hasn't received appropriate benefits or the right amount of benefits under workman's comp can file an **appeal** with the Iowa Workman's Compensation Commission.

Withholding

A variety of **taxes must be withheld** from the pay of an **employee**, including **federal income taxes and social security taxes, state income taxes, and state unemployment insurance taxes**. The business is required to hold these funds and then periodically deposit them and report them to the government. The government views the responsible parties as agents of the government, when performing these duties.

Social Security taxes must be withheld if:

- **Total farm wages** (including non-cash wages) are **over $2,500** for the year; **or**
- The **cash wages of any one employee are over $150** for the year.

Unemployment, federal income tax, and state income tax withholding must be taken out, as well. Additionally, the employer must provide a **paystub** showing the deductions and other specific items withheld, and the employer must mail the employee a **W-2 form** at the end of the year, to file with his or her own income tax return. The only exemption from these requirements is for children under 18 who are employed by their parents in a non-corporate partnership or LLC farm business.

If your help qualifies as an **independent contractor**, is an individual (not a partnership, corporation, or LLC), **and you pay over $600** to them during the calendar year, you must follow **IRS 1099 reporting rules** and send the contractor a **1099 form** at the end of the year, to be filed with his or her own income tax return.

When it comes to collecting income taxes, the IRS is definitely not swayed by the name you decide to give to the business relationship you have with your help. Instead, **the IRS uses a 21-point checklist** to help it determine whether the relationship is that of an **independent contractor or** is an **employer-employee** relationship. The overall theme of the checklist, however, is the same as in other legal arenas: The IRS is looking to determine the **degree of control** that you exercise over the work that is being performed by the help.

Minimum Wage and Overtime Pay

If you hire workers who are classified as **employees,**, then you could be subject to the additional requirements of the Fair Labor Practices Act of 1938, providing for a **minimum wage** and **overtime pay.** More than 500 "man days" (labor for at least 1 hour) per quarter must be worked on your behalf.

Generally, as long as fewer than five employees are present or it is a ranching situation, this act will not be triggered for minimum wage and overtime pay (The worker's spouses, parents, children, stepchildren and siblings do not count towards the calculation). Further, if the employee is **your family member** or engaged in **range production of livestock**, **no federal minimum wage** rules apply.

Payroll can be paid at different rates (biweekly or weekly), but the issue of **overtime** pay comes into play if the employee goes **over 40 hours in a 7-day calendar week**, regardless if it is in one pay period or two. Employees must be paid **time-and-one-half their regular hourly rates** of pay for hours worked in excess of 40 per week.

> **Note**: *Even if you have a policy of no overtime hours, you'll still have to pay overtime pay if an employee actually works the hours (with or without your knowledge), and the work benefits the farm.*

Employees who are **"agricultural workers"** are **exempt** from the **overtime** pay provisions, but before you decide not to pay the higher wage, be sure the employee in question truly qualifies as an ag worker.

> *For example, a worker sorting cattle for 10 hours/day is clearly an ag worker who isn't entitled to overtime, but the worker you use to sell fruit at a roadside stand for 10 hours/day would be entitled to overtime pay.*

You can encounter serious legal problems, by failing to keep and maintain records of the names and permanent addresses of temporary agricultural employees, dates of birth of minors under age 19, or hours worked by employees. As costs rise for labor, more and more operations, even small ones, need to resist any and all temptation to skirt around the requirements of the IRS or federal wage laws. You have to keep a constant eye on these laws, because some of them can change dramatically from year to year, influenced by politics and economics. The penalties for non-compliance are far worse than the burden of compliance.

> *The bottom line on this is to hire a bookkeeper or seek legal advice to keep yourself informed about the current state of these regulations.*

Failing to withhold when you should have been, or worse yet, telling your employee you have withheld and not turning it over to the government, can land you in lots of tax trouble that is hard to shake, including the possibility of being charged with a crime.

OSHA

The federal **Occupational Safety and Health Act (OSHA)** covers the majority of workers in Iowa. It does not cover the self-employed, farms where only immediate family members work, or places covered by other federal agencies and laws.

Children and Agricultural Employment

Both state and federal laws cover employment issues, including those involving **child labor**. You must follow the more restrictive law. The federal reach is broad, and while some exemptions exist to federal law coverage, the better and safer policy is to follow them both.

Working Your Own Children

Parents may work their children on their farms as they see fit, without violating child labor laws. In addition, the children may work **without restrictions**, except that the child may not be made to do **hazardous work** until **age 16**.

> *Note:* When the parents are using a business entity to operate the farm, this exemption is not clearly still available.

Work Hours and Duties

Under federal law, minor children who work in non-agricultural employment cannot be under 14 years of age, and are subject to the following basic rules, many of which turn on the age of the child laborer:

- Children aged 16 years or older can perform non-hazardous duties, with unlimited hours;
- Children aged 14 and 15 years cannot perform hazardous duties, work in manufacturing jobs, or work in mining, and they cannot work during school hours. They can work acceptable jobs:
    - Up to 3 hours/day on school days, up to 8 hours/day on non-school days, with a total of up to 18 hours/week, when **school is in session**;
    - Up to 40 hours/week, when **school is not in session**.

Children in **agricultural employment** may work:

- Up to 14 hours a week (in two-hour blocks) when school is in session; or
- Up to 20 hours a week (in maximum of four-hour blocks) when school is out.

In addition, children over the age of 14 may **de-tassel**, from **June through August**, with **no restriction on hours**.

> No matter how eager the child, don't ignore the work hours limitations for minor workers. Both **employers and parents** who allow a child to work in **violation of the child labor laws** may be punished by **fines**, or **jail time**, or both.

Teen-aged employees may drive a car or truck on farm property, operate garden-type tractors, clear brush by hand, hand-plant seeds or plants, weed, hoe and water plants, care for poultry and horses, pick produce, and help with milking operations. As a general rule, **minor children** (under the age of 18) **cannot** be employed to work in any of **these agriculture-related industries or tasks**:

- Logging;
- Power-driven woodworking machines;
- Power-driven metal punch machines;
- Slaughter;
- Meat packing or rendering plants;
- Circular saws;
- Band saws;
- Wrecking and demolition;
- Roofing;
- Excavating;
- Operating forklifts, backhoes, or cranes.

Hazardous Work

Essentially, *14- and 15-year-olds may do non-hazardous work*, and those *over age 16 may do hazardous work* in the agriculture industry. Hazardous work would include:

- Operating tractors over 20 horsepower (PTO);
- Combining; Mowing; Corn- or cotton-picking;
- Trencher or earthmoving equipment operation; or
- Being in stall with a bull, boar, stud horse, or a sow or cow with newborn offspring.

If the child is *under age 16*, he or she *cannot* work:

- Felling, bucking, stacking or loading timber;
- Working from a ladder or scaffold; or
- Transporting or applying NH3 or handling Category I toxic ag chemicals. (See ALSO 29 CFR 570.71(a)(1-11).

The Department of Labor is active in seeking to restrict this list further, and you should consult with your attorney or the Department of Labor to find out the current Ag Hazardous Occupation Orders to ensure your operation can safely employ your youth employee.

If you have a minor employee, ensure you have his or her full name, address and date of birth. If at all possible, make a photocopy of his or her driver's license and a second form of ID.

Becoming a Better Boss

Communicate Effectively

Being a good boss primarily requires the employer to learn effective communication techniques, which boost not only efficiency but also morale in the employer-employee relationship. Recognizing that the leader and the led are only two portions of a puzzle with several pieces, you must also consider the message and the goal, when communicating with employees. Employees want goals, and if they are not clear on what your goal is, they will substitute their own understanding of the goal. When the goals don't match, conflict often results.

> *For example, envision a day just before your spring planting, when your employee reports to work at the usual hour of 6 a.m., and expects to leave by the usual hour of 2 p.m., having made plans to meet her husband at home to prepare their own equipment for spring planting. Suppose further that you haven't told your employee about your powerful desire to spend that day moving your equipment to the field, in hopes of calibrating all the electronics, hurrying to be ready to plant at the first opportunity, when the crop insurance planting window opens up. Your goal is to make sure you are running hard the first available day, and you personally view this prep day as critical to get it all done, regardless of how long it takes. You expect your employee to stay late and pitch in the extra effort, along with everyone else, but you haven't communicated that plan to her. It's probably not hard to imagine that, as mid afternoon-approaches, two very different sets of expectations are brewing, which can create conflict and which could have been avoided by cluing the employee in at the start of the day or the beginning of the week on the things you, the employer, wanted to accomplish.*

Organize and Delegate

On your organizational structure, it is extremely important to understand how far your "aura" of control goes. In most organizations, about five or six people are the most that should report to one person. It is interesting that the lowest level of leadership in the military is a team, which is four- or five-soldier element, lead by a team leader. Battle- and time-tested are good litmus tests for any recommendation.

If every one of your employees reports directly to you and you have more than five employees, you probably need to reassess.

Be Fair, But Firm

In dealing with problem employees, discipline needs to be consistent and follow the same procedures, or it will not be perceived correctly. Employees are often irritated and have their morale damaged by a lack of realistic expectations, a lack of clear guidance, improper or incomplete training, or the refusal to delegate authority to the actual decision make-.

If employees are not performing, make sure to DO SOMETHING about it. Much like an unattended flesh wound, ignorance is not bliss. Until you address this issue, it will have an impact on the business, the workers' happiness and the workers' effectiveness.

As an employer, you want to be friendly and fair, but you simply cannot be perceived as a "buddy" to any of your employees.

As you examine your work environment as a leader, some key concepts to consider are:

- Get rid of the thought, "I can do it better and quicker."
- Delegate the results, not the method, unless the method is crucial to the success. Frequently, pliers and Vise Grips can get the job done equally, unless you are a Vise Grips salesperson.
- Delegate every decision down to the lowest-ranked employee capable of making the decision. Remember, you can delegate authority, but not responsibility. Once you have delegated a task, DO NOT EVER take it back, unless somebody or something (like profits) is about to be measurably hurt.
- All employees capable of delegating a task should remember that concept as well. Lead from the front.
- Acknowledge the work, no matter how trivial it might seem. We all want to feel like we are contributing to the team. However, avoid pandering and baseless praise. A simple acknowledgement goes a lot farther than empty rhetoric.

13 FARM LEASE BASICS

A lease is an agreement or contract, granting permission to use another's real estate or personal property for a set period of time, in exchange for money or other consideration. All leases bear basic similarities to one another, so some of the issues that you need to focus on will be similar with any lease. On the other hand, there are also major differences between leases of farm acreage, leases that involve a farm house and buildings, and leases of personal property, like farm equipment. In dealing with these differences, you will encounter issues unique to each type of lease.

Farm Acreage Leases

Farm acreage leases to tenant farmers are vital to many farm operations. Whether you are the landowner or the tenant, some simple rules should be kept in mind with farm land leases.

Get it in Writing

While it is still not uncommon for people to base land leases on verbal agreements, modern farm operators in today's business environment are always well-advised to **put the terms of a real estate lease into writing**. Written leases prevent misunderstandings between the parties. Make sure **both** parties **sign the lease**.

> NOTE: Do your best to make sure **successors in interest** (heirs upon death) on both sides understand the terms of the agreement, as well, to avoid the kinds of quarrels that can arise, when one party to a lease dies.

Important Lease Terms

A good, written farm property lease can contain a wide variety of very specific terms regulating the relationship between the parties and the manner in which the land may be used, but there are some basic terms that are crucial to every farm property lease:

- **Parties.** Ensure that all intended parties to the lease are named and adequately identified by the inclusion of their addresses or other unique identifying information.
- **Property Description.** Ensure an accurate description of the leased ground is included.
- **Lease Term.** The length of the lease term should be clearly-stated.
    - *Note:* A real estate lease can be **up to twenty years long** under Iowa law, but if it is **longer than five** years, the lease has to be **recorded**, just like a deed or a mortgage would, in the property records office.
- **Renewal Terms.** Include provisions allowing for any renewal of the lease and for notice of intent to renew (or not renew).
    - *Note:* A good farm property lease should also establish agreed-upon compensation for any fall fieldwork completion, in the event of nonrenewal of the lease.
- **Lease Price.** Whether your agreement involves crop-sharing, fixed-cash, flex-cash, or some other arrangement, your lease price should be spelled out in writing. **Reporting Requirements.** You should also discuss and include any reporting requirements, including **what** must be reported, along with **when** and **how** the tenant must make those reports.
    - For example, does the tenant have to provide grid sampling, yield monitor data, weigh wagon results or test plot results to the landowner? Can the landowner ask the cooperative how many bushels of grain were delivered?
- **Default.** Your lease should include a list of actions that count as defaults in the terms of the lease, specifying whether part or all of the listed defaults can be cured or waived by the other party.
- **Miscellaneous Provisions.** Miscellaneous provisions can include just about anything legal that you'd like to include as an important term of your lease. With farm tenants, common provisions include **indemnity clauses** or **hold-harmless agreements**, requiring the tenant to pay any damages that are assessed against you, if you are sued by someone or cited

by the government, based on something the tenant has done on the land.
- **Notice.** Include notice provisions, to specify how and when to give notice of default, notice of intent to terminate the lease, or any other notice needed to make the terms of the lease work.
- **Termination.** The lease should include procedures for terminating the lease, either voluntarily or involuntarily (like when there is a default).

Termination of Farm Property Leases

When **terminating** a lease, **Iowa Code** requires adherence to proper **notice**, and failure to follow Iowa laws regarding notice to a farm tenant may result in a renewal of the lease under the current terms:

- If you lease out **more than 40 acres**, you have to provide **notice** of termination to the tenant by **September 1**, or the lease **automatically renews** for the following year;
- Farm tenants who are leasing parcels of **less than 40 acres** enjoy **no such statutory protection from termination** on short notice. What this means is that these tenant farmers could have those "small parcels" taken away from them at anytime, unless they have **strong, written lease terms** to protect their interests.

Possession and Title to Growing Crops

Tenant farmers who review their leases may note that if they have been noticed off (terminated from renewal) properly, **March 1** is likely the **last day of possession**. Every day after that, the tenant may be assessed a liquidated damage payment to the landowner.

Tenants with crops still in the ground may not be able to harvest until after March 1. Each respective party (and their legal counsel) most likely has different beliefs about what the result should be there:

- Landowners believe tenants must abandon the crop left (which the landowner most likely plans to harvest and keep);
- Tenants believe they have as much time as they like (perhaps even after spring planting on the acres that the tenant DID renew on).

Neither side is entirely correct. This issue has been before the Iowa Supreme Court already, in a case where weather prevented the tenant from making a timely harvest. He did not renew the lease. That spring, the landowner refused access to the tenant's harvest attempts and instead, turned cattle and hogs out on the ground to consume the crop.

> *The Iowa Supreme Court declared that a matured crop belongs to the tenant, subject to the landowner's lien (if filed correctly). Maturity doesn't matter if the crop is severed from the ground, but the question turns on whether or not the crop still draws sustenance from the soil. However, abandoned crops are not treated the same. Abandoned crops become the property of the landowner and can be disposed of however they like.*

No clear guidance from the court is available to distinguish matured, non-severed crops from abandoned crops. However, common sense can help. A couple of stalks of corn in the corner of the field left, or maybe even a partial row left to help with snow drifting, can likely be declared abandoned by the tenant and taken by the landowner. Some would call that a blonde corn maze. Conversely, 20 acres left in the field is still property of the tenant, who has a reasonable right to harvest in peace.

The Landlord's Lien

A landlord's lien used to be superior to other creditors' claims. Changes in the law in the last several years no longer give landowners priority over other liens, if the lien is not timely filed.

A landowner who rents out ground and doesn't get all of his or her money upfront needs to file a UCC-1 statement with the Secretary of State, just like the bank and other folks, in order to protect is position for payment. The filing needs to be made within 20 days of possession by the tenant or earlier, if the tenant's lease authorizes it.

Liability for Tenant Activities

When is a landowner legally liable for harm that is caused to others by activities that a lease tenant conducts on the leased property? For example, a tenant who spreads manure or pesticides on the property might create a nuisance that affects a neighbor, who then wants to sue **you,** because you have more assets or better insurance against which to collect. Will you have to pay? What can you do to protect yourself from liability?

Landowners would be wise to consider the **Iowa Supreme Court ruling** in *Tetzlaff v. Camp and Pangborn.* In that case, Pangborn rented crop ground to Camp, who spread manure on the crop ground. Camp made a habit of revving up the tractor and letting the manure drift close to the nearby Tetzlaff house. Tetzlaff brought suit against both landowner and tenant, claiming nuisance, trespass, and negligence. There was little doubt, under existing Iowa law, that the landowner would have been liable for surface spreading manure near someone's home, *if* he had done it himself, but other Iowa law also said that, as a general rule, a landowner is not liable for damage caused by the acts of a tenant.

However, while the *Tetzlaff* Court did stress the general rule that a landowner is not responsible for tenants' acts, the Court found that a **landowner** who **renews** a lease **with notice** that the **tenant's prior use** resulted in **nuisance** may be **liable for the tenant's nuisance**.

The Court first asked whether the landowner would be liable if he had been the one carrying on the activity that is being complained about (i.e., in this case, whether the activity would constitute a legal nuisance). If so, then the Court adopted a test for landowner liability which asks:

- At the time of the lease (or in this case, the renewal of the lease), did the landowner either **consen**t to the activity or did he **know or have reason to know that it would be carried on**? **and**
- At the time of the lease (or renewal), did the landowner **know or have reason to know that the activity would necessarily involve or was already causing a nuisance**?

If the answer to both questions is yes, then the landowner could be held liable for the tenant's nuisance activity.

How does all of that affect what you do with your farm property leases? In practice, landowners should review leases with an eye towards seeking **indemnification** and **hold harmless agreements** from any tenant who accepts **manure** under a manure-management plan or manure-easement arrangement, because you face at least the potential for legal liability to third parties for any nuisance created, when a tenant uses manure as part of the operation.

Pricing Leases to Tenant Farmers

When you are **pricing leases**, some **flexible, nonstandard arrangements** can be made, which essentially lets the landowner in on some of the profit that can flow from **swings in the market**. This concept is called "**flex leasing**." Generally, the tenant and the landowner agree on a **base price** and on **trigger points, set by third-party standards** (like posted county price or crop insurance price rate), which may result in additional payments to the landowner.

> *For example, actual price multiplied by actual yield, which is divided by a base price multiplied by a base yield, will result in per acre rent payment that is likely to reflect some of the upward or downward movement in the market.*

Renting the Farm House and Buildings

When you decide to rent out a farm house and accompanying buildings and acreage, you are entering a separate profession: Residential Landlord. Residential tenants have rights that are very different from those of tenants who are renting bare ground. If disputes arise, judges are simply not as sympathetic, when you wear a landlord's cap and not your seed corn cap,.

In common with the tenant farmer land leases discussed above, several basic points should never be ignored with residential tenant leases:

Get it in Writing

A rental agreement in writing, signed by the landlord and the tenants, should always be required. While the laws of Iowa do not require a written rental agreement if the lease period is for less than one year, it would be reckless and just plain foolish not to get a rental agreement in writing for every single agreement made, regardless of the length of the lease.

Important Lease Terms

- As with the acreage leases discussed above, a written **residential lease agreement** should outline every important aspect of the agreement, including: The term of the agreement (i.e. the length of the lease);
- The amount of rent;
- The monthly due-date for payment of the rent;
- The amount of the security deposit (In Iowa, it cannot be more than two months' rent);
- Name and address of the manager or landlord;
- List of which utilities are paid by which party;
- Any special requests or requirements by either party.
    - *These could include terms limiting the number of occupants, assigning responsibility for mowing and snow removal, or listing maintenance that either party plans on having finished prior to occupancy. If the tenant is to be responsible for property maintenance, the lease must say so.*

Residential Security Deposits

The security deposit that you require on a residential lease cannot total more than two months' worth of rent, and it must be kept intact, in a bank account separate from personal funds. Within 30 days of termination, the landlord must return the deposit to the tenant, unless there are damages to the property and the landlord takes proper steps to collect them against the security deposit.

> **NOTE**: *It is generally a good practice to do a **walkthrough** before a tenant moves in and prior to the tenant leaving, to identify damage.*

If there are damages for which part of the deposit is retained or unpaid rent, the landlord can keep the appropriate amount of the deposit only if he or she:

- **Submits a written statement** to the tenant, specifying **why** the deposit was kept; **and**
- **Allows** the **tenant** to **inspect** the property and **submit a statement** of damage.

As a landlord, if you don't provide the written statement to the tenant, explaining why you did not return deposit money, you forfeit the deposit and any rights that you have to that money.

It is the responsibility of the tenant to provide a forwarding address where the deposit can be sent. The tenant's failure to do so can result in the tenant forfeiting any right to the deposit.

Habitability

As a landlord, it is **your legal responsibility** to provide the property to the tenant in a **habitable condition** and to **maintain the habitability** of the premises. This means making any needed **repairs** and ensuring the proper working order of all **electrical, plumbing, sanitary, heating, ventilating, air-conditioning, and other facilities**. If the tenant is to be responsible for the maintenance of the property it should be so stated in the rental agreement.

In the event the landlord fails to provide a habitable residence, the tenant has a right to terminate the agreement. If the tenant chooses to continue the agreement and make any needed repairs, they have the right to deduct the costs of those improvements from the rent.

After the rental agreement has been signed, the landlord may adopt new rules as long as they are in writing, they apply to all tenants living on the property, and their purpose is to create a better and safer living environment.

Inspecting the Premises

Unless there is an emergency, the landlord must give the tenant at least 24 hours' notice of the intent to enter a residential dwelling to inspect it, or for any reason other than an emergency. The tenant **must** let the landlord enter the dwelling if the tenant has received a fair warning that the landlord will do so or in the case of an emergency.

> *For example, if you see water seeping out of the house in the general vicinity of the bathroom, you may reasonably suspect a water leak, which is an emergency, and you can legally enter the house right then, without providing 24 hours' notice. On the other hand, if you're simply curious to see whether your tenant's housekeeping skills are up to snuff by your standards, you must provide the notice.*

Tenant Obligations and Terminating the Lease

In addition to paying the rent on time, a tenant must keep the premises as clean and safe as possible, including disposing of all garbage and other waste. The tenant must do all that is possible to keep appliances and other facilities in good working condition.

Generally, a tenant cannot use the premises for anything other than for housing. Any other uses must be approved by the landlord. The tenant must also notify the landlord of any extended absences from the home.

Non-Payment of Rent

The tenant must pay rent when it is due. When and ***if a tenant fails to pay rent*** in a timely manner, your ***first step*** as a landlord will be to ***serve*** a ***three-day notice to pay rent or quit (leave the premises)***. If another three days then passes with no payment of rent, your ***second step*** is to begin the ***eviction process***.

A written notice must be ***personally served***, hand-to-hand, so the tenant cannot claim that a legally-required notice was not given.

> NOTE: Your best bet for providing provable personal service is to hire a process server, contact the local sheriff, or at the very least, have an impartial third party deliver the notice.

On the other hand, if you've served a three-day notice, and the tenant has showed up within the three days and paid the ***full rent, plus any necessary associated costs and fees*** that came out of your pocket, then you must accept it and allow the tenant to stay. If it happens again, it is important to note that any time a tenant is late with the rent, a new three-day notice to cure or quit must be served.

If you allow the tenant to remain in the property without paying rent for 30 days, you take the risk that you could lose your ability to file a ***forcible entry and detainer action***.

However, a claim for the ***rent*** can still be made in ***small claims court***.

Other Breaches

If the tenant breaches the lease terms in some way other than failure to pay rent, the ***landlord must personally serve the tenant***

with a seven-day notice, indicating what can be done to conform to the agreement, and the landlord ***cannot terminate*** the lease ***for at least seven days after service***. If the tenant ***remedies*** the breach within seven days, the agreement cannot be terminated. If the tenant commits a substantially similar breach within six months, the landlord can evict without giving an opportunity to cure, but a seven-day notice of your intent to remove themj will still be required.

> **NOTE**: Personal service of a written notice means that someone hands the notice, in person, to the recipient, and it helps avoid any claims that notice was not served. As with other notices, your best course is to hire a process server, contact the local sheriff, or at the very least have an impartial third party either deliver the notice.

Terminating the Lease

When the landlord gives ***written notice of termination and notice to quit***, the documents must be ***served*** on the tenant by either personal service or by sending notice by certified or restricted certified mail.

To terminate a rental agreement, whether the party terminating it is the landlord or tenant, notice of termination must be given an appropriate amount of time, as set forth in Iowa law, before the anticipated date of termination:

- If the tenancy is ***week-to-week***, ***ten (10) days' notice*** must be given for termination.
- If the tenancy is ***month-to-month***, at least ***thirty (30) days' notice*** is required.

If a ***lease is for a one-year period or more*** and ***notice of termination is not timely*** given to the tenant, the lease will be ***automatically renewed***, meaning that the tenant will continue the lease on the same terms as before, except that the tenancy will then become a month-to-month tenancy. Therefore, if a one year or longer lease term is coming to an end, and the landlord doesn't want to continue renting to the current tenant, it is important to make sure that notice of termination is given to the other party at least 30 days in advance of the termination date.

Forcible Entry and Detainer

Once the lease is **properly terminated** by one of the previous procedures, the landlord can serve a **forcible-entry-and-detainer action (FED)**, which is a court action to evict a tenant who **refuses to leave voluntarily**.

Service of Notice

Notice of the FED must be served on the tenant, but if a process server or sheriff is unsuccessful in serving the papers after two attempts, then service can be made by certified mail with restricted delivery (if signed for by tenant). If none of that is successful, the notice can be attached to the front door of the residence (but only if two previous attempts at personal service were unsuccessful).

> **NOTE**: Using mail is not recommended, because a 2009 Supreme Court case has made this unconstitutional for at least one type of landlord action, casting doubt on its validity in other landlord cases.

Filing the FED in Court

Among the papers served is a 3-day notice to quit (leave the premises), and the landlord must allow the full three days to expire, before filing the FED with the Clerk of Court for Small Claims.

> **NOTE**: If you have previously served a three-day Notice of Nonpayment of Rent, a further three-day Notice to Quit is not necessary, in order to evict the tenant for that non-payment.

After you've filed with the Clerk of Court, a court hearing will be set. The **hearing date** must be set **at least three full days after the service of FED, but not more than 7 days after the FED was filed with the Clerk**, leaving a small window of time for scheduling the hearing, but getting the action over quickly. FED actions move so quickly because the law favors a quick resolution of issues involving real estate.

The FED Hearing

At the court hearing, the **only question** will be whether the tenant has a **right to remain** on the property; the FED court will not be a forum for airing disputes that don't affect that right to remain. A FED and Writ of Removal do not result in money damages for past rent due or property damage. If there is back rent due, money damages, or property damage, the landlord should initiate a small claims action.

The **tenant can appear at the FED hearing to contest** the eviction. Some tenants do, and some tenants don't, but the tenant's appearance or lack of it affects **how fast you can take possession** of the rental property:

- If the **tenant appears**, but has no defense, then you will be entitled to possession within **three days** from the hearing.
- If the **tenant does not show up**, you will be entitled to **immediate possession**.

If the tenant shows up offering cash, the landlord need not take the money and can demand any sum in order to dismiss the FED. Once the three-day cure period has expired for nonpayment of rent, the landlord is under no obligation to accept any further money from the tenant. However, the parties can negotiate an agreed judgment for possession and can come to agreement on a specific date when the tenant will move out.

Writ of Removal

If the **tenant** appeared and lost at the hearing, but **refuses to leave by the end of the three-day period or move-out date set by agreed judgment**, your next move is to seek a **Writ of Removal**.

> **NOTE**: If the hearing falls on a Tuesday or later in any given week, the landlord will be unable to obtain a Writ of Removal until the following Monday. A sharp landlord will recognize that pretending to give the tenant until midnight Sunday to move out will not compromise the landlord's legal position in the slightest, but it can look to the tenant like the landlord is "negotiating" (which may help curb the tenant's level of indignation, cutting down the likelihood of additional trouble while this tenant moves and generally avoiding bad publicity with other potential tenants)

The Clerk of Court will issue the Writ to the **Sheriff**, who will visit the rental unit, and the **Sheriff will appear on an agreed date**

to supervise the tenant's forcible move-out, with the following conditions:

- The landlord must supply the workers; and
- The landlord must supply boxes, bags, etc.

To protect yourself, you should either ***videotape*** the move-out or take ***photographs*** as you go along, including pictures of the tenant's personal property after removal. If items are expensive, it could be prudent to take photos before you ever touch the objects, as well, to avoid claims of unreasonable damage.

The tenant's possessions can only be removed to the ***public right-of-way***. Under NO circumstances should the tenant's possessions be left inside the property or taken to an offsite storage unit.

Self-Help

Self-help is ***never*** an option for the landlord. You ***cannot*** simply enter the premises and start moving the tenant's things out to the sidewalk, unless you have been through the appropriate legal steps to evict the tenant. The ***landlord must pursue an FED action*** and obtain an ***Order for Possession***.. If the tenant is still in possession of the rental unit past the date the court sets in the order, the landlord must obtain a ***Writ of Removal***.

If the ***tenant abandons*** the rental property, the law gives you the right to seek new tenants. The first tenant's rental agreement is considered to be legally terminated on the date when the new tenants sign a lease.

A Landlord's Checklist

Here is a checklist, summarizing important matters that typically trip up a residential landlord:

- Always provide 24-hour notice prior to entering the rental unit, except in emergencies.
- In a month-to-month or longer lease, give at least 30 days' notice of termination of the lease. A one-year lease does not simply terminate; the landlord must give 30 days' notice if he

- or she will not be continuing the lease agreement, or it will renew automatically.
- A written agreement cannot be changed unless the changes are agreed upon by the parties. This includes an increase in rent.
- If the landlord wants to increase the rent at the expiration of the lease term, provide 30-days' notice of termination and rewrite and execute a new lease, with the new terms.
- Failure to pay rent should result in a three-day notice being served on the tenant in every situation. Do not let a tenant slide, or you could lose the ability to collect for that month.
  - Example: Your tenant fails to pay July rent, but you don't serve a three-day notice to quit. In August, the tenant again fails to pay rent, so you serve a three-day notice to quit, hoping to force payment of rent for both July and August. Your tenant will not be required by law to pay the July rent in order to cure the defect.
- When serving the tenant with any notice, do it in person with a witness, or hire the sheriff or a process server to do it.
- Get everything in writing and make sure all parties are aware of their responsibilities.
- If landlord is retaining any of the deposit, they are required to provide a written explanation to the tenant within 30 days. Failure to do so will terminate the landlord's rights to the deposit.

Leasing Farm Equipment

Farmers lag behind other industries in renting equipment instead of owning it (16 percent versus 32 percent), in spite of the many benefits of leasing equipment, which include deductibility of the payment, cash flow, keeping up with the latest technology, and not clouding the balance sheet with another asset and liability and attendant bank loan.

Many modern farm operations are catching on to the fact that leasing equipment can make sense, under the right circumstances. For example, equipment leases may be the best option for farm operations, in situations like these:

- When you only need the equipment for a short period of time or it will be obsolete in a few years;

- When your ability to deduct the cost of purchase is limited by income and other deduction rules; or
- When, at the end of a projected use period, the equipment will have low residual value.

Beware of lease-to-own contracts. If, at the end of the term, the piece of equipment can be bought for little to no cost or can be bought for a set price that is not related to its residual value, it may be treated as a disguised sale by the IRS. Other warning signs include having a lease period that exceeds 75 percent of the useful life of the item or having the lease payments equal nearly the cost of acquisition. The IRS has a rule, called the 20/20 test in a published revenue procedure to help it determine if the lease is truly a sale. The 20/20 comes from ensuring that 20 percent value remains in the equipment at then end of the lease and at least 20 percent of the useful life of the equipment remains at the end of the lease. Having the IRS determine how an item is treated for taxes is rarely a good thing for the tax filer.

14 MULTI-PERIL CROP INSURANCE BASICS

The **Federal Crop Insurance Act**, first passed in 1938, aimed to promote economic stability in agriculture, by offering producers access to crop insurance, but historically, participation was low, until the passage of the **1994 Federal Crop Insurance Reform Act**, the creation of the federal **Risk Management Agency (RMA)** in 1996, and the **2000 Agricultural Risk Protection Act**. The result has been a combination of additional subsidies and access to additional types of coverage, causing participation to rise dramatically. In addition, ag operations now have greater access to many insurance providers; currently, there are fifteen (15) insurance companies with federal approval to offer crop insurance policies.

Multi-Peril Crop Insurance (MPCI) is the only type of crop insurance available through the Federal Crop Insurance program, which aims to protect farmers against loss of production below a calculated coverage level, which is determined by using the farmer's actual production history. The farm operator cannot pick and choose which fields will create the production history (Just like family members the good and the bad all figure in the pool!).

Farm crop insurance is slowly replacing disaster-relief and similar farm program payments from the federal government, and its role will continue to grow larger in coming years, as the government seeks to make farm program payments compliant with World Trade Organization requirements and less costly to the strained federal budget.

Coverage

MPCI policies must be **bought before you plant**, and **one policy per county** protects the operator from **covered causes of loss**. While a variety of causes can result in crop loss, **MPCI plans** are written to cover only the listed causes of loss that are actually stated in each specified crop's **policy provisions**.

For example, covered causes of loss may include adverse weather, fire (excluding arson), insect plague, diseased plants, and revenue protection (a change in harvest price from the projected price).

Hail damage is a cause of loss for which you may have to purchase a separate policy, called **crop-hail insurance.** Crop-hail insurance is **not offered through the federal crop insurance program**. You have to purchase that type of insurance on your own, from private providers.

A critical term for determining **coverage levels** in crop insurance is the **APH (Approved Actual Production History Yield)**. The APH is equal to the sum of actual, proven yields, divided by the number of years in the database, up to 10. At least four years must be used, or a percentage of yield ("T") will be used to get the database up to four years.

A farm operator chooses coverage levels in **increments of 5 percentage points**, between 50 percent and 85 percent of APH. The result of APH, multiplied by the percentage selected, is the **production guarantee**. If a pricing feature is included in the policy, the policy will spell out how the price is determined.

Revenue Protection Plans

The **Revenue Protection Plan** protects against **lower yields, lower prices, or a combination of both**. It can also include a feature providing that if the harvest price is higher than the projected price, the revenue guarantee increases. The **minimum revenue guarantee** is based on the projected price, multiplied by the APH, multiplied by the level of coverage. If the harvest price is higher than the projected price, the harvest price will be used to calculate the final revenue guarantee. This will give the farm operator **upward price protection** in situations where production shortfalls will need to be replaced at higher harvest prices.

Revenue Protection Plans use **regional commodity exchanges** to establish the minimum revenue guarantee, the premium, and any replant or prevented planting payments. The **harvest price** comes from regional commodity exchanges and is multiplied by the actual yield to establish the **calculated revenue**.

Revenue Protection Plan with Harvest Price Exclusion

The **Revenue Protection Plan with Harvest Price Exclusion** is a policy that excludes the use of the harvest price in the determination of the final revenue guarantee, resulting in **no upward price protection**. It is available for Iowa crops of **corn, soybeans and wheat**.

Yield Protection Plan

The **Yield Protection Plan** provides coverage against **production loss.** It is available for commonly-grown Iowa crops — including corn, soybeans, and wheat — as well as other, non-Iowa crops. The Yield Protection plan establishes a level of protection in accordance with a **production guarantee,** which is determined by multiplying the APH for the unit by the level of coverage selected. The insured may normally elect coverage levels from 50 percent up to 75 percent of the APH, but in certain cases, the insured may elect 80 percent to 85 percent of the approved APH, in some cases.

15 PLANNING

It is estimated that 70 percent of North American farms will change hands by 2025. This does not just include ownership, but also who farms the land. This provides plenty of opportunity for American farmers who plan.

Farming is Becoming an Industrial-Style Business

Modern business realities are forcing farmers to let go of the concept that farming is a lifestyle that deserves special provisions. It is apparent that farming is considered a business to the non-farm sector, and unless farm operators learn to think like business owners, they will be consumed by those who do. Direct payments and counter-cyclical payments from the government will be under attack, and crop insurance will likely replace guarantee payments.

American farming has had three golden ages in the last 100 years:

- During the 1910s (when warring European countries shot each other into the stone ages, leaving the U.S. to meet demand for food in Europe);
- During World War II (when everyone wanted to get involved in shooting European countries back into the stone ages) and the period thereafter; and
- During the mid-1970s (again, when our competitors abroad couldn't meet demand).

A drive through farm country, with an eye to noticing when farmhouses were built, will show you that the constructions correspond with the timeline of America's golden farming booms. You'll see that lots of 1915 builds still dot the countryside, alongside plenty of post-World War II expansions and 1970s ranch-style houses.

Avoiding Boom-Time Pitfalls

Generally, when prices are high, a many businesses will make decisions that cause financial problems later, when the price falls. . Farmers who fall in this group tend to do the following:

- Expand their operation, by buying high-priced land and shiny new machinery.
- Defer the sale of commodities or payments, to escape the tax consequences.
- Get sloppy with personal spending and indulge in boats, trips, and nostalgia purchases, like restoring Grandpa's "H Farmall."
- Carry less in hard cash, instead planning to convert assets as needed and leverage existing assets against next year's crop.

When prices are high, the farm operator doesn't think much about the long-term wisdom of these actions. When the prices dive lower, the good-times decisions may be hard to maneuver away from.

Farm operators should take advantage of high prices by:

- Lowering expenses.
- Paying the tax on the operation's good times.
- Building cash for purchases of capital items when the slump hits.
- Resisting shiny-paint fever and the urge to get newer, faster and better equipment for comfort and ease, opting instead for increased profitability.

Tax Considerations

For the years 2011 and 2012, **long-term capital gains** (assets held for more than one year) are taxed at a **maximum tax rate of 15 percent** (**unless** you are selling collectibles or have depreciation recapture on real estate, when the maximum rate is 28 percent and 25 percent, respectively).

> *For example, if you sell land that you have held for more than a year, the maximum federal tax rate on this gain is 15 percent, whether your gain on the sale is $50,000 or $5 million.*

In Iowa, don't forget about **state income tax**. You need to **add this rate to the 15 percent federal rate**, to arrive at your **overall effective** *tax rate*. The state income taxes paid are allowed as a **deduction** on your federal tax return; however, this deduction may be **disallowed** in arriving at your **alternative minimum tax**. You may have a **possible additional deduction on your Iowa state tax return** for the sale of farm land in certain distinct situations and you need to check this out.

But remember, 15 percent is the **maximum federal long-term capital gains tax rate.** For those farmers in the *lower tax bracket, they may have long-term capital gains taxed at zero*. For all capital gains and qualified dividend income in the 15 percent or lower income-tax bracket, this part of the gain is taxed at zero.

> *For example, if your income from farming and all other non-capital gain income creates net taxable income of $20,000, you can have long-term capitals and dividend income of about $50,000, which will be tax-free for 2011 and 2012.*

Hobby Farm Rules

Those who are just beginning a farm operation, those who work "in town," or those who are slowly withdrawing from farming would do well to familiarize themselves with the **Internal Revenue Code § 183, "Activities Not Engaged in for Profit,"** occasionally referred to as **"The Horse Shelter"** or **"Hobby Loss Rules."**

> **IRC section 183** is designed to **prevent taxpayers from claiming business losses** (and thereby reducing income available for taxation) on activities the taxpayer primarily engages in for **recreation, entertainment and personal enjoyment**, rather than a legitimate business purpose. Specifically, **horse farms** and **cattle operations** of small sizes are eyed with greater scrutiny.

The IRS trains its Section 183 examiners, who may have no prior knowledge of farm operations, attempting to use manuals and policies to familiarize its agents with everything from the world of competitive show animals, to the distinction between registered and commercial herds of cattle. Several factors are considered by these examiners, and knowing what agents look at can help you make important decisions about your farm's business activity and record-keeping:

Factors Considered by IRS Hobby Farm Rules Examiners

The IRS agent training manual advises Section 183 examiners to consider calculating the volume of feed purchased versus animals sold, to ensure no under-reporting of income, such as cash sales.

Several factors are reviewed by the IRS, and each one is briefly examined below:

1. **Books and Activities Maintained**: The examiner will review the level of sophistication of the records, notably if the enterprise has a separate checkbook from the personal living expense checkbook of the taxpayer. The mere presence of records is not enough; the taxpayer must show he or she is relying on the records to make decisions and changes to the operation to make it profitable, not just to satisfy, for example, a breed association records-keeping requirement.
2. **Business Plan**: The examiners want to review a formal, written business plan, demonstrating realistic growth and economic forecast for the enterprise, that if successful, would result in a viable operation. Relying on occasional profits or windfall activities, such as only being profitable in the event of twin colts, fails to meet the concept of a solid business plan.
3. **Methods and Efficiency of the Operation**: The IRS will review the use of experts or specialists by the taxpayer in order to achieve profitability. A good example of this is documentation of Iowa state service programs, publications consulted, and demonstrable selection criteria for genotype of seed or breeding stock selected and retained. If the taxpayer has failed to heed advice to change operations without a justification (like lack of funds to change), this will cause concern on the part of the examiner. Likewise, if the taxpayer devotes little time to an activity but generates a large loss, it will attract scrunity.
4. **Disguised Expenses**: An example of this might include overzealous advertising via "vanity ads." This will attract an examiner's attention. Consider the true purpose of any advertising spent by the operation. An ad with a picture of a child and horse, wishing luck to the taxpayer's children in the upcoming horse show, is not viewed usually as a legitimate business expense.
5. **Potential for Increase in the Value of Assets**: If a business is showing a loss, but can demonstrate that its assets (like land) will increase due to the business activity over time, it may help appease an examiner's concerns of hobby loss. The

intent to capture the increase in value must be demonstrated as well.
6. **Taxpayer's Success in Other Activities**: A taxpayer with high profitability in a sideline restaurant, who annually loses large amounts on cattle production because of high expenses, will be scrutinized to determine if his best efforts are also being applied to the cattle operation. Additionally, a taxpayer with substantial sources of income have not fared well with the tax court.
7. **Pleasure Element**: IRS training manuals warn examiners not to be lulled by the argument that farming is a drudgery, though case law supports the concept that devoting hours upon hours to crop input, attending to calving and foaling at all hours of the night, and enduring the elements is not normally undertaken without a profit motive. And the Internal Revenue Service does not mandate that taxpayers cannot enjoy their income production. However, passion without profit paints the picture of an enterprise not undertaken for profit.

Showing a profit can help you avoid much of this kind of searching IRS analysis of your business deductions. A ***presumption*** in the law indicates that a profit once every few years, depending on the enterprise, shows the activity is engaged in for-profit enterprise. Consider this example:

> *A person who worked as an accountant for 20 years also operated a thoroughbred horse racing and breeding enterprise. After examination and a subsequent court case, it was determined that no business losses could be taken from the enterprise. The court looked at (1) No businesslike manner of activity, to include a separate checking account or records to determine profitability; (2) no changes designed to increase profitability; (3) failure to obtain personal expertise advice of experts in an attempt to make a profit; (4) no horse ever sold for more than $750; (5) the accountant had no experience in operation of any type of business; (6) the losses went on for 20 years; and (7) the losses shielded income from the accounting business.*

The lesson to take home for the night and weekend farmers is to:

- Make sure you have a separate checking account;
- Hit an Iowa State Extension seminar or a field day (and make a record of attending);

- Make a record of your consultations with herd improvement, crop consultants or area managers of service providers regarding your enterprise;
- Have a written plan on how you intend to make profit at your endeavor; and
- Consider how you can manage your taxes to show a profit once every five years or so.

Business Formation

As with all businesses, deciding the legal form that your business will take is a planning staple for the farm business enterprise. Legal business forms can include limited liability companies, corporations, or partnerships, among others.

Each legal business form has its own characteristics, offering different advantages for different business needs. For example, establishing a business entity allows for the formal transfer of partial interests in farm operations, sets up rules for how the next generation gets along, and may provide some tax benefits. One main purpose of business entities is usually to protect the business owners from personal liability for business debts. On the other hand, if done incorrectly, it may cause a significant tax issue and other problems, which the "Do-it-Yourself" LLC or "Form your own Corporation" kits sold on the internet likely won't identify.

Basically, all business formations are legalized lies , creating alter egos to spread risk. Without the law saying a corporation can do certain things, it is no more a real person than your son's make-believe playmates. However, since the law recognizes business entities as "legal fictions," your lawyer can help you select one of these beasts for your business, picking one that comes with certain built-in advantages and disadvantages.

Common Business Entities

If you sell services or goods, you own a business. If you're the only owner and you don't have it organized any other way, it is called a **sole proprietorship**. It dies when you die and is an alter-ego of you (think Clark Kent and Superman). You take all the rewards, but you pay all the taxes and expose yourself to all the risk. These small businesses sprout and die like annual plants, as they can rarely grow without adding a more formal structure to take advantage of employees, access to capital and tax incentives and breaks.

Partnerships are another default type of business form that happen when **two or more people** combine resources for a project. Each partner is liable and responsible for the actions of the other partners.

> *For example, Joe and Sue begin milking together. Sue orders feed in the partnership name that Joe didn't want delivered. Joe and Sue are both equally responsible for paying for the full amount of the feed bill. Either one can be sued in court, if the feed bill isn't paid, and the debt can be satisfied out of either one's personal holdings, like real estate, bank accounts, or other assets.*

A good way to prevent this personal liability is a ***limited partnership*** filing. This allows parties to limit liability by designating assets that are subject to the debts of the partnership. It also puts creditors on notice that Joe or Sue's off-farm income from a job may not be available to pay the debts of the partnership. The partnership's profits or losses pass through to the partners on either a predetermined percentage or in accordance with their contributions to the partnership. Further, in a limited partnership, some partners' risk can be limited to what they contribute to the organization.

C-Corporations, also called "C-Corps" or just "Corporations," were once favored by the estate and business planning community. The advantages of C- Corps include limited liability to share owners, tax deductions not available for other types of entities, and a low tax rate on the first $75,000 of income made. However, the C-Corp has some built-in disadvantages — particularly if it owns highly-appreciated land.

> *For example, a C-Corp owns farm land with a low $1,000 per acre basis. When it goes to sell the ground at $4,000 an acre, not only will it have to pay capital gains tax on the transaction, but then also when that profit is distributed to the shareholders via dividend, that dividend is subject to tax again. Conversely, if the land was owned outright by the individuals, only the capital gains tax would be paid. Also, C corps cannot pass losses on to the owners.*

Target, Wal-Mart, and publicly-traded companies are C corporations. Any number of people can hold stock in a C corp. However, in *Iowa*, only *"family farm corporations"* (where the majority of the property and income is from the agricultural sector) can own Iowa real estate, unless it is put to nonfarm use soon after it is acquired.

S-Corporations ("S-Corps") meld the limited liability of corporations with some favorable partnership principles, like taxation. S-Corps pass through the losses and gains to the shareholders like a partnership and are not subject to the double tax problem that C-Corps may have, but they do not enjoy other tax advantages that a C-Corp can offer. In addition, you may only have a certain number of members of an S corporation, and they have some limits on what fringe benefits the majority owners can receive.

Limited Liability Companies ("LLCs") are another blend of partnership and corporations. They require fewer formalities than a corporation, but they still provide liability and asset protection to the members. For tax purposes, they can be treated as a partnership and pass through the gains and losses, or if only one person is in the company, he or she can elect to be treated like a sole proprietorship for taxation, while keeping some liability and contract responsibility protections.

Selecting a Business Form

Now consider how to use these forms to the greatest advantage when planning a **business transition**. The business form you select can be used in conjunction with **estate planning** tools to produce favorable results for both the elder generation and its heirs. Here's an example:

> *The elder owners of a farm could form an LLC, which would both rent the ground from the owners and also operate the farm. An on-farm heir could work as an employee of the LLC for a few years, ensuring that the heir both operates well with the parents and also acquires the necessary skills to successfully continue business into the future. The parents can choose to either gift or sell an interest in the LLC to the heir, using buy-sell agreements to control who could buy out whom, for how much, and when. The elder generation would have some income, from rents and from the proceeds of any sale of an interest to the next generation. The estate plan could include*

> off-farm heirs receiving non-farm assets and allowing the on-farm heir to inherit the farm. If no non-farm assets exist, valuation mechanisms can be put into place to ensure that the on-farm heir can buy the farm ground from the estate at a reasonable price. This funds the off-farm heirs' estate bequests and avoids the on-farm heir simply inheriting new landlords (the siblings) when the parents die.

Sound complex? It certainly can be, and unless you are truly familiar with the rules and confident that you know what you're doing, you should **consult a lawyer, an accountant, or both**, before making decisions about the business form you select and how to use it. **Failing to follow the rules can be dangerous**. Here's a real-life example:

> The IRS was recently successful in challenging the tax return of a farm couple, during the year they transferred the farm operation to a corporation. While the couple set up a corporation, they failed to deed their business property over to the corporation or make the farm program payments payable to the corporation. After they received the payments in their own name, they transferred the funds to the corporate account. On their taxes, they claimed the income under their own operation and then claimed an expense for transferring it to the corporation, reducing the self-employment tax to under $500 for $250,000 of gross income. They followed that with a corporate income tax filing showing the income and offsetting it with the following year's expenses. Instead, the IRS established that the farm couple really owed self-employment tax on the funds, and was able to raise their tax liability to over $28,000, plus penalties.

Had the couple established the corporation and correctly followed the rules for transferring the land and the government payments to the corporation *prior* to receiving the funds, a different result may have been achieved. The key, like most things in life, is to know the rules and follow them.

Business Entity Formalities are not "Mere" Formalities

Business entity formalities (or "corporate formalities") are **requirements imposed by the same statutory laws that create the business entities**. In the case of a C-Corporation, for example, the state may require a certain corporate structure, a real set of officers, a real board of directors, real board meetings with formal minutes, and annual filings with the state, among other things. Other business forms require other formalities, according to the statutes that apply to those entities.

What happens if you don't follow business entity formalities? The answer is simple. ***You don't get the benefits*** that you were looking for when you chose the entity. A C-Corporation that doesn't have officers, doesn't keep minutes of its meetings, or misses its annual filings may be considered by the law to be a ***sham corporation*** and may not protect its owners from ***liability*** or provide desired ***tax benefits***. It is absolutely essential that you follow required corporate formalities and not mix "hats," when you have one of these separate legal creatures under your control.

If you have more than one business entity under your control, it is equally important that your two companies ***deal with one another "at arm's length,"*** and not mix ***assets*** or engage in informal ***contractual relationships***. Here's an example of how all these formalities can matter:

> If Farmer owns both Hog LLC and Grain, LLC, it would be wise to have a written agreement between Hog and Grain to establish at what price Hog buys Grain's corn to feed Hog's hogs. And they should have separate checking accounts and a separate list of equipment. This will help prevent Hog LLC's debt from becoming Grain's debt or Farmer's personal debt. This is called ***"piercing the corporate veil."*** That is "lawyerese" terminology for a method used by hungry creditors to call " bullshit" on your multiple business creatures, in order to force you to pay poorly-performing Hog enterprise's bills from your profitable hardware store's assets.

A word on ***liability***: No matter what corporate structure you choose to use, you cannot protect yourself from yourself. If you choose to tell an employee to climb on a grain bin in a lightning storm, and he gets hurt and sues you personally, you are personally responsible for your act, no matter whether you did it in your LLC, corporation, partnership, or pact with the devil. On the other hand, if you were in the right corporate structure, you might be able to avoid personal liability for your sister's order to operate the combine with faulty wiring, dry beans and a heat wave.

Farm Programs

Types of Farm Payments

To remove some of the volatility from farm operations, the government provides *five types of farm payments*:

- *Direct payments* are a government set amount, paid according to a farm's "base acreage." Base acreage is determined by establishing what percentage of the total acres is devoted to the crop that payments are provided for.
- *Counter-cyclical payments* are set based on a "target" price, which triggers payment when the commodity price falls below the target.
- Alternatively, the *Average Crop Revenue Election* program uses revenue guarantees based on a minimum price set by national averages and state yields.
- *Loan Deficiency payments* are based on the difference between commodity loan rates and the payment rate for the loan. This is a streamlined way of handling marketing assistance loans that are offered by the government.
- *Emergency payment programs* are triggered in crop failures. Most government program payments are income.

Losing your Farm Payments

However, you do not have access to farm program payments if you *run afoul of government rules*. You will likely receive a *notice of adverse action or determination* or a *notice of violation*. These are your warning shots that you are not doing what your government thinks you should be doing, regarding federal farm programs, and if you receive such a warning, your choices are:

- To continue to do what you want to on your property and no longer participate in the programs (along with potentially having to pay back any benefits you have received);
- To comply with the government's requirements; or
- To appeal the government's decision.

Appeals

Appealing a government adverse decision can be accomplished in several different ways. You may appeal to the *county- or state-*

level committees that, in theory, govern over the government officials assigned to your county. You can ask for reconsideration, go to mediation or file a formal appeal. The appeals are handled through a special administrative procedure which eventually winds up at a special ***"National Appeals Division" of the Department of Agriculture.***

What can you appeal? You may appeal any of these adverse decisions:

- NRCS technical determinations;
- Errors in documentation and calculations necessary to determine program eligibility;
- Errors in calculations and documentation to determine ability to repay FLP assistance,
    - Either in connection with loan servicing or a request for a new loan;
    - All matters relating to correctly applying regulations pertinent to an issue of fact;
    - Appraising security, except negotiated appraisals relating to primary loan servicing;
    - Whether a participant is farming in a farmer-like manner.

FSA is required to ***notify*** participants of adverse decisions. Those notification letters **must** contain the following:

- ***Background*** — A brief narrative explaining the reason for the letter;
- ***General Program Provisions*** — A statement about the program for which the participant filed an application, executed a contract, sought a determination, or the provision that brought about the need for an administrative determination;
- ***FSA's Findings*** — A general discussion of the pertinent facts based on specific references to either the application, contract, information submitted by the participant, or other relevant information or evidence that can be and is specifically cited and referenced in the decision letter;
- ***Discussion*** — A narrative explaining the findings together with the general program provisions;
- ***Determination*** — FSA's decision based on the general program provisions, findings, and Discussion; and
- ***Mandatory Language*** for adverse decision letters.

The FSA has a handbook that outlines what mandatory language it must include, yet it sometimes fails to do so.

For most people, the rules regarding appeals and FSA requirements are complex and truly murky. Finding and using experienced legal representation is highly advisable when telling the government it is wrong – especially if your farm payments are riding on the outcome.

16 REAL ESTATE AND FARMING

Farming by its very nature depends on real property. Learning the legal lingo and the basics of acquiring, using, and disposing of real property can be as crucial for a farmer as learning the difference between diesel and gasoline.

Abstract and Title Opinion

If you are considering buying a piece of property, your first move, before you sign anything or pay out the purchase price, should be to consult a lawyer about getting a proper **title opinion**. Banks will require you to do this, because lenders use the whether you have clear title or not.

A title opinion is a formal legal opinion about the validity of the seller's ownership interest in a piece of real estatessued by an abstractor with a abstract company who has examined a variety of records relating to that property and has put together an **abstract of title**. An abstract is a sort of written history of everything that has created a possible legal impact on the ownership of the property, and to develop an abstract, an abstractor will research deeds, mortgages, releases, death records, liens, lawsuits, judgments, marriages, divorces, taxes, and other legal records. The attorney reviews this abstract to issue the opinion. A title opinion is like a book report on that historical story.

Types of Deeds

Property ownership is most often conveyed or transferred by either a Warranty Deed or a Quitclaim Deed. A warranty deed is the best kind to get, if you are a buyer, purchasing a piece of real estate.

With a warranty deed, a seller "warrants" good ownership of the property, free and clear of any outside claims or faults. If something should come up later that questions the validity of good title to the property, the seller remains liable to the buyer for that.

On the other hand, a seller who gives a quitclaim deed simply abandons ("quits") whatever ownership interest or claim, if any, that the seller has in a piece of property. The seller may have good title, or the seller may have none. The seller makes no warranty of ownership, and a quitclaim deed puts the risk of surprises on the buyer.

Warranty deeds are the preferred method to take title, when purchasing real estate. However, while the quitclaim deed may sound risky, this kind of deed is perfectly adequate in some situations, it is actually the standard deed used in certain circumstances, and it can even be used to cure some existing problems with title to a piece of land.

> *For example, when two people marry, one of them can purchase property in his or her own name, and the property is held in that name, but the other spouse acquires rights, called dower/curtesy rights, to inherit that property if the owner spouse dies. When the two divorce, and an item of real estate is awarded to one spouse, the other must sign a quitclaim deed, abandoning his or her interest in these dower/curtesy rights. The quitclaim deed is the proper deed to use for this purpose.*

Property laws affecting good title can be quite complex. Before accepting any deed, no matter what it's called, a buyer should consult an attorney, who can determine the validity of the seller's ownership interests after researching and preparing a title opinion.

Types of Real Property Ownership

Joint Ownership of Property

You can own a piece of real estate jointly with another person or persons. Joint ownership means that each co-owner owns a given interest in the entire piece of real estate – usually, each owns a one-half interest, but not necessarily.

What does it mean to co-own property equally with someone? Even if two people each own an equal interest in a piece of property, there is no physical "half" of it that one can fence off and keep from the other. Instead, each co-owner has the right to use the whole property, along with the right to one-half of the proceeds, if the property is sold (If the joint owners cannot agree on how to use the property, there is such a thing as a "partition" lawsuit, filed in court by one of the joint owners, in which a judge is asked to put an end to the joint ownership and force the sale of the property).

There are different forms of joint ownership, and the rights and obligations that result from them depend on the language that is used in your deed. Here are different forms of joint ownership, and a few notes about the rights of the co-owners in each situation:

- **Joint tenants with rights of survivorship (JTWRS)** – If one co-owner dies, the surviving co-owner(s) automatically own the deceased person's interest. If you are the survivor, you need only file an affidavit when the other co-owner dies, in order to take good title to his or her portion.
- **Tenants in common (TIC).** This form of joint ownership does not include survivorship rights for the co-owners. If one co-owner dies, his or her last will could control what happens to his or her interest. If a co-owner dies, a probate estate must be opened, in order for title to be transferred.
- **Life estates.** In this arrangement, a person has ownership rights in a piece of property that last only for the length of time that the person is alive. A life interest is not perpetual, and it is generally followed by a "remainder" interest granted to some other person(s).
  - **For many years, a life estate to the surviving spouse with a remainder interest to the children was a cheap, effective way to pass real estate without a lot of complex will-drafting.** It allowed a widow to continue to benefit from the land, while ensuring that the children ultimately took title to it. Further, the life estate ensured that a second spouse and that spouse's children didn't "get their hands on" family assets, usually farm ground. The elder generation essentially got to behave as if the ground was still entirely theirs (rent collected, taxes paid, military and homestead exemptions applied) until their deaths.

Property rights are said to be like a bundle of sticks. Each aspect of property (right to use, responsibility to pay taxes, mineral rights, wind farm rights) is one of the sticks in the bundle. Owners or co-owners with full ownership rights (called a "fee interest") hold the entire bundle of sticks. Under a life estate, one person holds onto the right to occupy and use the property along with the responsibility to pay the taxes (the life estate holder). Another person(s) (remainderman) hold(s) the rest, and when the first person dies, those "sticks" transfer to the second person(s).

The remaindermen do have some rights, even while a life estate holder is still alive. For example, the remaindermen can prevent "waste" of the value of the property, like logging trees from the property or the demolition of good quality buildings, but enforcing these rights can sometimes turn into a litigation battle.

Problems with Life Estates

Court rulings and modern realities make life estates less appealing than they might seem. First, while the transfer occurs upon the life estate holder's death, the remaindermen cannot take those sticks without clearing a **Medicaid lien** on the property. The value of the life estate holder's interest is figured just prior to his death. This can mean that despite transfer of substantial interest in the farm prior to death, a life estate holder on Title 19 can be made to pay back part of monies advanced for care in a long-term care facility.

Second, the **tax basis** for a life estate property is established at the time of transfer, not at death. If it was not a sale with a retained life estate, then the remaindermen get the transferor's presumably low basis in the property, not the higher "stepped up" basis that they would have received had the property been transferred via probate proceedings. This means that more **taxable income** will be recognized, if and when the remaindermen sell the property.

It gets even more tangled and snarled when folks retain a life estate to their spouse, then a life estate to their children and make the grandchildren the remaindermen. This can run afoul of **federal gift tax law**, because the gift to the grandchildren is a gift of a future interest, and no **gift tax exclusion** is available for such a gift.

Thus, the life estate may still have some applicability, but its use as a quick and easy way to avoid planning should be fading.

Easements

Sometimes, one piece of property acquires rights, known as **easements**, to **make use of or cross over** another. Easements can be for travel, access, drainage, noise, smell, or any number of things that could otherwise burden the property subject to the easement.

Easements are just another stick in the bundle of sticks that make up property rights. These rights can be given freely, or they can be taken from the other property, as a matter of right.

Agreed easements are easy to understand, but many people have never heard of proscriptive easements – the kind that can be taken from another property, without agreement.

> **Example: If you cross your neighbor's pasture long enough, you may acquire a right to travel across it via a proscriptive easement, if the neighbor didn't give permission; or you may acquire a permissive easement, if he did.**

Easements need not be **recorded**, but it is a great idea to do so. A good easement contains the legal descriptions from the recorded deeds of both the properties involved, and it should be written as specifically as possible, with an eye towards preventing future problems.

For example, an easement to allow "access to the pasture" is vague. Does it mean access to drive cattle across the parcel? What about farm equipment, when the pasture is torn up? Consider that an easement that is 15 feet wide was probably great in 1948, but now is probably unduly small to allow passage of larger, modern farm implements. The easement should address who has to maintain the property and how costs get shared.

The best course is to have an attorney prepare a written easement. A poorly-written easement that leaves room for confusion is likely to lead to conflicts later that will have to be settled in court, and that situation will produce much larger attorneys fees, other costs, and potential business losses, for all involved.

Property Rights in Marriage

In a marriage, it takes only one person to buy property, but two to sell. Even a spouse whose name is not on the deed of title nevertheless has an interest in the property that arises from very, very old laws of marriage and inheritance, called **dower/curtesy rights**, designed to protect a person's expectation that entering into marriage with someone would automatically mean that he or she would gain the support and use of the other spouse's property.

These ancient property rights of dower and curtesy continue to play certain roles in modern property law, but for your purposes, the most important rule to remember is this:

Even if only one spouse's name is on the deed of purchase, both must sign a deed to transfer the property out to some new owner.

- If you're married and you're selling a piece of real estate, your spouse **must sign** the deed.
- If you're buying real estate from a married person, his or her spouse **must sign** the deed.

Purchasing property

All **property purchase agreements** need to be in writing, or they are not enforceable. All binding agreements follow a simple formula of **Offer + Acceptance + Consideration (payment of the purchase price) = Binding Contract.**

> For example, "I will buy your farm today," is not a valid contract. Nor is "I will buy your farm for $10,000 someday."

Everyone gets stuck on the price, the CSR, and FSA maps to create an offer. What are often missed are fine details, like **allocating the purchase price** between buildings, dwellings, well, tile, fences and improvements, and dates of possession. Unless an agreement is made to the contrary, if you buy real estate, the **crops growing** on it pass with it.

- From the buyer's standpoint, a portion of the purchase price should be allocated to the residence (which cannot be depreciated), buildings, fences and wells (which are depreciable to the buyer), and then a portion to the bare ground.
- From the seller's standpoint, it would be best to have as much of the purchase price, as possible, allocated the residence. This is because the seller receives favorable tax treatment as a capital gain (and in some cases, could be completely excluded from gain tax). The seller wants no more assigned to the buildings, fences, tile and well than they have remaining

on the depreciation schedule, as the excess assigned to those items will be treated as ordinary income, which is not as favorable as a capital gain.

Adverse Possession

When does "the back forty" become "the back **forty-two**"?

The subject of acquiring title to property by **adverse possession** always seems to generate interest and discussion, but when the facts and the law are peeled back far enough, adverse possession is fairly rare. Adverse possession determines **acquisition of title (not use) to property** by possession. Because the law presumes possession is under regular title, the doctrine of adverse possession is strictly construed. That means it is not going to be something the court wants to find and a close case will go to the record titleholder, not the claiming party.

The concept of adverse possession is based on the **10-year statute of limitations**, and a party claiming title by adverse possession must have **clear and positive proof** that establishes **hostile, actual, open, exclusive, and continuous possession, under claim of right or color of title, for at least 10 years**. Each of these **required elements** for adverse possession presents a separate hurdle:

1. **Hostile Possession.** Hostility refers to words or acts that show a person claims a right to use the land. Where no formal declarations of intent are made, hostility can be demonstrated by acts characteristic of an owner, rather than those of a mere user, such as maintaining and improving land. Interestingly, payment of taxes is not essential to the acquisition of title by adverse possession. Permissive use of land is not considered to be hostile or under a claim of right, even if it continues over a long period of time, so if your neighbor knows you cut through his yard and waves to you when you do it, the hostility is defeated.
2. **Actual Possession.** The claimant need not live upon land, enclose it with fences, or stand guard. It is enough if the claimant treats the property like his own ground of similar nature (but this means that the conduct to claim a building is different from the conduct required to claim a wooded lot). A claim of ownership may be shown by receiving the rents,

issues, and profits of the property, by improving it, or by paying for insurance on the property.
3. **Open/Notorious Possession**. This requires proof or showing that the true owner **should be aware** somebody else is claiming the ground. Erecting signs and buildings, or cropping the land, are all things that should indicate to the true owner that someone is using the ground.
4. **Exclusive Possession**. **A mixed, shared or scrambled possession is not exclusive** and will not ripen into title. Again, when you cut across the neighbor's yard and he uses the same route, you are not establishing possession. If you fenced him out, however, that would be exclusive and for your benefit.
5. **Continuous Possession**. This part requires a **type of claim** and a **holding period** of 10 years. The two types of claims are **Claim of Right** or **Color of Title**.

    a. A **Claim of Right** is described as "I think the land is mine." **Good Faith is essential**. If the person claiming adverse possession didn't believe the land was theirs, then the Claim of Right basis for adverse possession fails. An example of this can be found in a case in which a woman attempted to claim a strip of her neighbor's land by adverse possession. The court denied her claim because she knew it was not her property, even though she had treated the property as her own for 30 years.
    b. **Color of Title** is a **document-based claim**, summed up as, "somebody gave me a document that says the property is mine." An example could be a mistyped deed, title, or last will, which leads you to believe you own part of the neighboring property, a title document which appears to grant you title, but in reality is no title. Such a document, taken in good faith, gives you a toehold to a claim of adverse possession. So if you take a deed for the southwest quarter of the southwest quarter of Section 6 and live on it and hold it for ten years, even though you were only sold the southern half of the southwest quarter of the southwest quarter of Section 6, you may have a claim.

6. **For Ten (10) Years**. This is a simple math problem. Consider a scenario in which you have maintained an abandoned railroad right-of-way as your own for years and otherwise meet all the elements for adverse possession. Perhaps, under Claim of Right, you thought the land was yours when the tracks were pulled up, or under Color of Title, the strip was conveyed to

you, when in reality, it belongs to an out-of-state investor. Five days before the end of the 10 years, the investor's summer intern comes out and says, "Thanks for taking care of that. We are putting in a new ethanol spur line here, so you can take your last crop off." The ten-year period is most likely not met and you are out of a strip of land.

Sound simple? Consider this real-life example from a court case:

> *A disputed strip of land was between parcels owned by two hunting clubs. The disputed land was included in the plaintiff's title description, as demonstrated by a survey performed more than 10 years before the plaintiff brought suit to quiet title. Both parties provided evidence of use of the disputed area by hunters. Both owners placed deer stands in the disputed area and both removed stands placed by the other party. Although a barbed-wire fence existed in the disputed area, the fence had not been maintained by either party and was not continuous.*

The court held that the defendant failed to prove exclusive use of the disputed area; therefore, title remained with the plaintiff as record titleholder. Here, the defendant should have spoken up loud and often, if it believed it had title to that disputed strip. Waiting ten years to raise a fuss about the issue probably weighed heavily against any claim it asserted on the property

Acquiring title through adverse possession is a lot harder than just claiming that the fence post was moved 10 years ago and now you own what's inside it. You'd make a better investment of your time and money having conversations with the neighbors, to buy their property if you want to buy it, and otherwise, to ensure that everyone knows who owns what.

Tax Planning in Property Transactions

Capital gains tax is generally lower than ordinary income tax rates. The tax is computed on an amount equal to the difference in your **basis** in the property and the amount you get when you sell or dispose of the property. There are variations, but that is the essential rule.

Basis is a tax term of art. In general, it means the amount you pay for a property you purchase, but there are a variety of things that can push your basis up or down, thus affecting your ultimate tax liability when you get rid of the property. For example, if you acquire property by some means that is not a purchase, you may get a **transferred basis,** related to the cost paid for the property by the previous owner, or you could get a **stepped-up basis,** related to the value of the property at the time you receive it.

A **step up in basis** is a concept that allows a person who receives property from an estate to pay capital gains tax on only the difference between the value at the date of the donor's death and at the date of sale. On the other hand, if the property is gifted to the same person while the donor is still alive, the cost basis that the gift-giver paid for the property **transfers** to the new person..

- For example, if a farm was bought in 1950 for $300 per acre and given to the next generation during the owner's lifetime, in 2011, when the market value was $10,000 per acre the gift donee would get a transferred basis of $300 per acre. If the donee sold the property at current market price, he would pay capital gains tax on $9,700 per acre.
- On the other hand, if the next generation inherited the property in 2011, the recipient would get a stepped-up basis of $10,000/acre. If the recipient sold the property for $12,000 an acre in 2014, only $2,000 per acre would be subject to capital gain tax.

The IRS allows you to **delay paying capital gains taxes** on a sale by conducting a **"like kind" exchange**. This is a process where you give up one piece of property and acquire another, similar property in exchange. The basis from your old property is transferred to the new property and you delay paying capital gains tax until you sell the new property. However, with careful tax planning developed by an attorney or accountant, you can exchange into another property, and then hold that until death, when your heirs will receive a step up in basis and pay lower capital gains tax.

When you pay for property, you need to use a real estate agent or an attorney to close the transaction. This ensures all the terms of your agreement are enforced, and that the transaction is properly recorded. The closing agent should provide you a settlement statement showing how the purchase price, along with credits and additional expenses, are allocated.

Visitors

Premises Liability and Care of Your Property

In Iowa, in order to avoid possible liability for injuries caused to someone else by a condition that exists on your property, you are required to take **reasonable care** of the property. If you have a **dangerous condition** on your property (sink hole, pool of tar, abandoned leaning building) you need to **take steps that a "reasonable person" would take to safeguard against it injuring someone**. This can mean fencing off the area, placing signs, or removing the hazard.

Trespassers

Can you shoot the guy stealing your cattle? Probably not. Again, you must take reasonable care to avoid having conditions on your property that could injure even a trespasser. However, since you don't expect, or **foresee,** intrusions by trespassers, "reasonable care" in that situation is less demanding than it is, when you have expected or even invited visitors.

Iowa actually has the leading case in the nation on defense of property and premises liability for injuring a trespasser. In the case, the landowner's property was invaded a number of times and items were stolen. The landowner set up a "spring gun" that shot a crossbow bolt into the intruder the next time he entered the house. The intruder sued the landowner and won. "Reasonable care" has often been interpreted to mean that you can't set up a situation on your property that constitutes a trap for a trespasser.

Fence Law

In Iowa, a farmer has the responsibility to fence in livestock, but if an animal causes damage because of poor fencing by neighbors, the neighbors can't recover. If the animal's owner has the poor fence, he is the responsible party. Taking time to inspect your fence (and note it in a journal) is a good plan for livestock owners.

A landowner, even one who doesn't own livestock, can be compelled to erect a fence upon written request of an adjacent owner. Also, a landowner can be made to build or maintain a fence on ground where a fencing agreement is in place. A written fencing agreement is best, and where that doesn't work, the owner can request an order from township trustees. The township trustees will order the fence equally, regardless of who benefits most from its installation.

A *legal fence* is:

- *Three rails* (10 feet apart for posts);
- *Three boards* (6 inches wide, with ¾-inch thick posts, no more than 8 feet apart);
- *Four high-tensile wires* (4 parallel, *coated, stee*l, smooth ASTM wires, not more than two rods apart and at least 40 inches h*igh);*
- *Three barbed wires* (36 iron barbs of two points each, or 26 barbs of 4 points, no more than two rods apart with two sta*ys between posts,* or one rod apart without stays, and a top wire between 48-54 inches);*Four wires, two sm*ooth and two of 25 four-point barbs, two rods apart with two stays between posts, or one rod apart wi*thout stays (with* all having not more than 20 inches or less than 16 inches from the lo*west run t*o the ground and a top run between 48-54 inches).

A *tight fence* requires the addition of woven wire to restrain sheep and swine, with posts not more than 20 feet apart.

If *livestock escape* three times in a 12-month period and trespass on the same landowner, the landowner can make a request to compel the animal owner to make a fence. If the complaining landowner is a neighboring landowner, the complaint may result in the complaining landowner having to put up fence as well. Establishing a *written and recorded fence agreement* is a surefire way to prevent this drama. A well-written fence agreement spells out who pays for what, and what happens if someone doesn't pay for what they are assigned.

Zoning

Zoning ordinances, whether adopted under city or county zoning authority, *do not apply* to land, farm houses, farm barns, farm outbuildings, or other buildings or structures which are primarily adapted, by reason of nature and area, for use for ***agricultural purposes***.

Agriculture is the art or science of cultivating the ground, including crop harvesting and livestock rearing and management. According to the Supreme Court of Iowa, farming is a continuum which begins with the planting of the crop and continues through its cultivation and harvesting. Hog confinement facilities and grain storage facilities also qualify for the agricultural exemption from zoning regulations.

Excavating

"***One Call***" is Iowa's system to ensure that most ***underground network*** activities are not damaged by ground work. The telephone number is (800) 292-8989.

Iowa law doesn't exempt farm operators from the obligation to call Iowa One Call 48 hours prior to performing any of the following operations:

- Drain tiling;
- Terracing;
- Any operation that penetrates the soil more than 15 inches in depth, including chiseling, subsoiling, or ripping;
- Digging or driving a post at a new location.

> **NOTE:** *A farm owner who complies with One Call is not responsible for any damages incurred while operating the farm in the normal course of operation, unless the farmer intentionally damages the underground location or acts with wanton disregard.*

A One Call employee will mark any underground activities with appropriately-colored paint or flags, for the following types of devices:

- Red: Electric
- Yellow: Gas/Oil/Steam
- Orange: Communications
- Blue: Drinkable water
- Purple: Reclaimed, irrigation or slurry water
- Green: Sewer

NOTE: Private facilities may not be marked and the farm operator needs to be aware of those privately dug lines (including propane lines) when conducting operations.

Wind Energy

Wind energy agreements involve easements for placement of towers, gathering stations, roads to the towers, and for the shadows and flickers caused by the turbines. Not all wind energy agreements are created equally. Some energy companies insist on privacy and attempt to keep wind-farm neighbors "in the dark," so to speak, about the details of one another's compensation plans.

As a landowner, you will want an agreement that is fair, when it comes to what you are paid, and the risks and limits that are placed on your own use of your land. Watch out for agreements that are too one-sided or pro-power company, with few rights being reserved that would allow the landowner to respond to future changes in use and pricing of wind energy.

Value

Knowledge of the potential of the wind project is key to understanding value. One way to get a lot of information easily is to obtain a copy of the ***Power Purchase Agreement*** between the wind company and the electric company, which will have the ***electrical sale rate*** and the ***estimated production capability***. An inflation factor should be built into any kind of fixed-payment arrangement.

Conditions of use can also affect the value of the contract. Look to the agreement to see if the power company has any duty to actually put up a tower, or if it is simply locking out competitors from entering an area. A hard-fought right to a percentage of the production generated is not worth anything, if no duty to actually produce wind energy on the site exists.

Landowners should also be aware of ***Renewable Energy Credits (REC)*** - an important, but sometimes overlooked, second source of revenue from a wind project. In some cases, the power is sold to one source, and the REC can be sold to an entirely different company, which may need the REC, to offset the non-renewable energy it is creating from other power production plants. ***Changing federal*** *and state laws are steadily increasing the value of REC to energy companies and thus increasing the value to a sharp landowner.*

If helping your local community is of greater value to you than the money to be gained from the contract, make sure that the company you're doing business with will actually be helping to meet that goal. For example, a national company will not likely have an impact on the local economy, as the profits from wind generation will flow to its shareholders. Some communities have created locally-owned wind production projects as a way to keep the value-added resource of wind production dollars in the community. For some, this distinction may be critical in deciding with which company to sign.

Tying Up your Land

The *length of the wind-energy lease* should be considered, with a view to the fact that land-use decisions made now may have a long-term impact on the availability of the land for later, profitable use by you or your heirs. Most leases are for a period of 20 years or longer, but some attempt to reach into perpetuity.

A well-drafted agreement may contemplate *many different types of easements*, some lasting the length of the agreement and some temporary. For example, the agreement may contain a defined construction easement area that is different from the area to be used once the tower is established or different from the easement for access to and from the tower. All of these easements are like little contracts within the larger agreement, and all are important areas to review.

Other considerations to keep in mind include:

- Who pays the property taxes on the newly constructed site?
- What impact does the wind tower have on use of the remaining ground? (Building restrictions and CRP eligibility come to mind.)
- Choice of law (where can you sue to enforce your rights and what state's laws apply).
- What happens when the site is abandoned, or is destroyed by Mother Nature or acts of negligence or sabotage?
- Premises liability for injuries to third parties should be assumed by the company, and the company should be required by the terms of your wind energy agreement to provide insurance for this liability.

17 REGULATION OF AGRICULTURE

A virtual alphabet soup of **federal environmental laws** regulates many of the activities that are a normal part of farming and other agricultural production. **Iowa state laws** can cover similar areas and also address areas not regulated by the feds, such as the killing of game animals, the neglect of domesticated animals, protection of other agricultural operations (like bee-keeping), and even the mowing of your weeds.

The major federal laws are contained in the U.S. Code (USC), including the **Clean Water Act (CWA), the Clean Air Act (CAA), the Comprehensive Environmental Response Compensation and Liability Act (CERCLA), Resource and Conservation Recovery Act (RCRA), the Migratory Bird Treaty act (MBTA), Federal Insecticide, Fungicide and Rodenticide Act (FIFRA), and the Endangered Species Act (ESA)**, **plus** the hundreds of **federal regulations** published in the Code of Federal Regulations (CFR) that help flesh out the details of these laws.

But it doesn't end there. For example, just take regulation of **animal disease issues.** More federal statutes, like the Meat inspection Act, the Egg Production Inspection Act, and the Poultry Inspection Act, and even more federal regulations, combine to address animal disease issues.

The federal **Environmental Protection Agency (EPA)**, other federal agencies, and **Iowa's Department of Natural Resources (DNR)** cooperate to enforce these federal and state laws, and enforcement efforts are becoming increasingly strict.

Penalties

What happens if you fail to obey laws affecting agricultural production? The result varies with the particular statute involved, but in some cases, you could be looking at real problems. In addition to penalties like the loss of federal subsidies, many of these state and federal environmental laws use **criminal penalties, like fines, forfeitures, and even jail time**, to strongly encourage your voluntary compliance with the law.

This means that ignoring the law could cost you a lot of money, possibly the loss of your property, or even time spent sitting in a federal or state penitentiary. Even if you disagree with the purposes behind some of these laws, you must take them very seriously.

Spotting Legal Issues in Agriculture

In some cases, avoiding liability under these laws can be tricky. Here are a few basics about the major laws and the kinds of activity and operations that can trigger them. Becoming familiar with the issues could help you foresee potentially bad situations and take action to prevent legal problems before they get started.

Ag Operations Affecting Water

The **Clean Water Act (CWA)** is the main cudgel in the arsenal of the EPA, as the agency seeks to regulate discharge of **pollutants**. Iowa uses the Department of Natural Resources, following rules of the Iowa Environmental Protection Council, to implement CWA rules, along with state laws protecting water quality.

These laws don't just deal with issues you might expect, like **spills of chemicals** or **run-off** from **pesticides**, **herbicides**, or **commercial fertilizers,** but they also cover issues like application of **manure:**

The **EPA** regulates **manure runo off** by requiring an **National Pollutant Discharge Elimination System (NPDES) permit**, if a point of the source of pollution can be found. Liquid manure has been considered a **point source**, as has manure spreading equipment. **Non-point sources** of pollution include introduction of pollutants from scattered sources.

Generally speaking, Iowa law also regulates discharges into state waters, excepting treated sewage and industrial or other waste, produced by operators with state permits. **Spill reporting must be completed within six hours of discovering the release**.

The CWA also protects **wetlands** by regulating **fill and dredge activities**. The EPA continues to assert that it can control all wetland fill and drain activities, but court rulings have prevented total control. Rather, the EPA can control if a nexus exists between the wetland and a navigable body of water. An exemption for normal farm activities (plowing, seeding, cultivating, minor drainage and harvesting) exists, if the activities are part of an established, ongoing operation.

Essentially, you cannot drain wetlands that have not been previously farmed, but you can continue to farm already-drained wetlands, as long as the activity remains in the "normal farming" definition. However, the regulations dealing with previously-used wetlands are complex, and if you're in doubt about your legal rights to use this kind of property, get authoritative advice before you do it, not later.

Penalties for violating the CWA include fines that can range from $2,500 to $1,000,000, per occurrence. Some fines compound on a daily basis. This adds up fast.

Ag Operations and the Clean Air Act

The Clean Air Act (CAA) provisions that affect agricultural production in Iowa are enforced through Iowa's DNR. **On-farm incinerators, grain storage operations** and **open field burning** are all subject to regulation, as well as potentially large-scale **anaerobic lagoons in feeding operations.**

Grain elevators with more than 2.5 million bushels at a terminal or **storage elevators** with more than 1 million bushels must control emissions and gases from loading and unloading grain.

Open burning is **only** authorized by the DNR via **exemption or variance**. Your **burning location** must be at least a quarter-mile from any inhabited building (other than your own), livestock area, wildlife area, or water source.

Exemptions (which are not valid during burn ban times) exist for **disaster rubbish, trees and tree parts, landscape waste, and residential waste for families not in multiplexes**. Burn barrels at livestock buildings that are not near a residence are at risk of being fined, because if what you're burning cannot be classified as residential waste, then no permissible use can be found to support the burning.

Also exempted are **paper and plastic pesticide or seed corn bags**. However, **pesticide containers** with mercury, lead, selenium, beryllium, arsenic and cadmium are limited to 50 lbs. a day, or one day's accumulation, whichever is smaller.

Burning buildings associated with crop production is allowed in some cases, as long as:

- **You remove chemicals and asphalt shingles**; and
- **You obtain permission** from the local fire authorities. Obtaining permission before burning is not only crucial, but wise, because the burning rules get tighter and tighter every year.

Will I get in trouble for creating dust? While *Iowa* law requires "*fugitive dust*" to be controlled, *agriculture is currently exempt*. While the **EPA** has once again said it will not regulate **dust emitted by farmers harvesting** or conducting other farm operations, this decision is a matter of federal policy. With changes in federal administration can come changes in such federal policies, and the EPA may try to use this law, designed to ensure national emission standards, to regulate farming operations in the future.

Ag Operations and Hazardous Chemicals

CERCLA

The **Comprehensive Environmental Response Compensation and Liability Act (CERCLA)**, more commonly known as the "**Superfund" Act**, addresses **disposal of hazardous chemicals**. Farm operations can run afoul of this by failing to report to the EPA when there is a **discharge or spill of hazardous chemicals**, like pesticides, insecticides, and herbicides, if the amount of the discharge is over a certain, **reportable threshold amount**.

Penalties for violating CERCLA can range up to $250,000, per occurrence, and some can be compounded **daily**. Again, the cost of a violation, versus the cost of complying with the law, can add up fast.

RCRA

The **Resource Conservation and Recovery Act (RCRA)**, also covers **hazardous waste disposal sites**. The **Iowa DNR** has similar provisions it enforces, even for **non-hazardous or "solid" wastes**. **Dumping** of just about anything, at a non-permitted site, is not allowed.

Exemptions can allow disposal of your own **farm buildings**, dumping of **farm waste** of the producer and burying of **dead animals** from that specific property.

When **disposing of dead animals**, the **Iowa DNR rules include specifications** that must be followed, as to the depth of burial, covering of carcasses, and the number of animal carcasses that can be disposed together.

Chemical Waste

If a farmer uses or disposes of federally-regulated agricultural chemicals or containers, the farmer is exempt from RCRA rules if the application and disposal follow manufacturer's guidelines, each container is triple rinsed after being emptied, and the rinse is dumped into the tank mix for application at approved rates.

Waste Oil and Tires

CERCLA, RCRA, the CAA, the CWA, and Iowa state laws control the dumping of **waste oil** and **waste tires**. These laws should be taken very seriously and followed closely.

Waste Oil cannot be placed into an un-permitted, informal dump, landfill, or waterway. Find a **waste oil collection site** and take care of it the right way. **Spills must be reported** to the EPA right away. Those who generate less than 25 gallons of waste oil in a month are **exempt** from storage regulations.

Waste Tires can never be burned or dumped on your property, in the river, or elsewhere. Take them to a **licensed tire recycling location**. The law does allow the use of used tires for **stream bank erosion control and culvert outlets**, and to **hold down covers on ag products**, like hay or silage.

If you plan to use old tires for one of these purposes, you should seek permission, to ensure that tighter rules later do not cause you *a headache. If you plan to use more than 250 tires, you MUST get permission.*

Underground Storage Tanks (USTs)

An **UST** is a *tank that holds regulated substances, including petroleum products, with at least ten percent of the tank being located below the ground*. **Exemptions** exist for farm tanks holding less than 1,100 gallons of motor fuel, home heating oil tanks, septic tanks, and some tanks in basements. **Spills** must be reported within 24 hours.

Fungicide and Rodenticide Act (FIFRA) and Pesticide Act of Iowa

The law requires that **pesticides** be **used and applied** in the manner approved on the label. **Containers** must be **stored, moved and removed** in a way that doesn't negatively impact the environment. **Pesticide applicators** need to have a commercial, non-commercial, private or public **license**. Some **exemptions** exist, for emergencies and operating on someone else's license.

Restricted-use pesticides must be applied by licensed applicators, who must keep **records** as to kind, amount, reason, date and places that restricted use pesticides are applied. These records need to be **entered within 14 days** of application and **kept for two years**. Within **30 days** of application, the person who hired the application must have a **copy** of the notes. These notes can be turned over to federal agencies without further orders.

Notes about application of restricted-use pesticides should include brand name, EPA number, total amount applied, size of area treated, crop to which they were applied, physical location, date (month, day and year), and the applicator's name and certification number.

Workers near ag pesticides need training and provision on how to protect themselves from exposure. Evidence of pesticide exposure on a property where the product is not used is strong evidence of **pesticide drift**. If confronted about this, take steps to document the evidence.

Special warning about pesticides and bees: If the label indicates a pesticide you're using is toxic to bees, a two-mile radius must be kept from any registered beehive, registered with the FSA. IF the application is to be within the two miles, the beehive owner must have at least 24 and no more than 72 hour notice of intent to spray.

Farm operations that store and use **hazardous chemicals** while conducting **routine agricultural practices** are **exempt from the Material Data Safety Sheet rules** that apply to others using such hazardous chemicals.

Animals

Animal control statutes can prevent **importation** of any animals, domesticated or wild, from abroad and from state to state. The states may issue state-level **quarantines**, and they have the power to order the **destruction** of animals, with **compensation** to the owner.

Wild Animals are protected by the **Fish and Wildlife Division** of the Iowa DNR. The **game laws** are many, and like every other citizen, a farmer is subject to Iowa hunting rules that address the killing of **game animals**. The fact that the farm provides the lion's share of the food for most of the game animals gives no special treatment to the farmer. Landowners may have extra hunting licenses for deer, but a farm operation is not required to get one.

Landowners have a right to **deer licenses** and a DNR program controls issuing **additional tags for crop damage**, but an agreement must be executed with the DNR. Documentation is the key. Taking the matter in to your own hands will not go over well with the DNR, and it may cause you to run afoul of other laws, as well. For example, carrying a loaded shotgun or other firearm in your combine is not a good idea. Aside from the obvious safety concerns about the potential for firearm accidents, your combine is a **motor vehicle** and the rules that control the use of motor vehicles apply to you, even though you are only going 5 mph.

When it comes to animals that belong to an **endangered species**, just about everyone knows that you **cannot shoot, capture, or kill** one of them. What doesn't jump out at you is that you **cannot modify the environmental situation or habitat** of an endangered species, which is considered the same as killing them. Even if one or more of these animals is killing your livestock, you are not free to kill an endangered species. Also, leaving out piles of grain as **bait** will create an illegal taking.

Wild animals belong to the state, but when you **hit a wild animal with a vehicle**, the state generally wants absolutely no part of the liability for them. This is a concept going back to the idea of the woods belonging to the King. Since the king is now the state, the state conveniently makes the rules so that it can control the harvest of animals, but avoid responsibility for the unplanned end of animals.

However, there could be a bonus: If the animal you hit with a vehicle is not endangered and is a game species, you may contact a DNR official for a "***salvage tag***" to harvest what is not embedded in your vehicle's grill.

Animal Neglect

Animal neglect is a state-level law that is gaining popularity with law enforcement and has become quite a social cause. Many concerned citizens will routinely call in questionable-looking animals, which may prompt a visit from the local law enforcement and the state veterinarian.

If your animals are not being properly cared-for, then the law allows removal of the animals, and the state can force you to pay the cost of removing and housing them. A frequent companion complaint is a failure to dispose of animal carcasses within 24 hours of death. In the winter in Iowa, this can be a no-win situation. Best practice would be to burn or compost the carcass, or at least stockpile and cover with lime to indicate that you are not just letting the animal decompose where it sits.

Noxious Weeds

Noxious weeds must be burnt, cut or destroyed by landowner and tenant alike. If you allow weeds to get out of control, an **order** that requires you to get rid of them will be sought and delivered via mail or process server. After that, if you still **fail to control weeds**, you'll find that someone will come and do it for you, at a premium price, equal to the **cost of the weed removal PLUS a twenty-five percent surcharge**, all **taxed against the real estate**. In other words, you'd be wise to make your own arrangements for effective weed control.

BIBLIOGRAPHY

Websites

(All Internet website materials remained current as of 12/31/2011)
Agriculture News, Commodity Markets & Prices from AgWeb, Powered by Farm Journal. Web. <http://www.agweb.com/>.
"Rules & Regulations - Livestock Farm, Building Regulations." *Coalition to Support Iowa's Farmers.* Web. <http://www.supportfarmers.com/rules-and-regulations.cfm>.
"Oil Spills | Emergency Management | US EPA." *US Environmental Protection Agency.* Web. <http://www.epa.gov/oilspill>.
"Office of Underground Storage Tanks (OUST) | US EPA." *US Environmental Protection Agency.* Web. <http://www.epa.gov/oust>.
Internal Revenue Service. Web. <http://www.irs.gov>.
Iowa Attorney General, Tom Miller. Web. <http://www.iowaattorneygeneral.org/working_for_farmers>.
Iowa Farm Bureau. Web. <http://www.iowafarmbureau.com>.
Iowa Department of Natural Resources. Web. <www.iowadnr.gov>.
Iowa Department of Transportation. Web. <http://www.iowadot.gov>.
"Rules and Regulations - Farmer Safety Initiative." *Iowa Department of Transportation.* Web. <http://www.iowadot.gov/farmersafety/rulesandregulations.html>.
Center for Agricultural Law and Taxation - Iowa State University. Web. <http://www.calt.iastate.edu>.
"Iowa Drainage Law Manual." *Center for Transportation Research and Education at Iowa State University.* Web. <http://www.ctre.iastate.edu/pubs/drainage_law/>.

Iowa State University Extension and Outreach. Web. <http://www.extension.iastate.edu/>.

IowaWorks - Integrated Workforce Delivery. Web. <http://www.iowaworks.org/>.

"Child Labor Law and Work Permits - Iowa Division of Labor - Iowa Workforce Development." *Iowa Workforce Development - Iowa's Employment Security Agency*. Web. <http://www.iowaworkforce.org/labor/childlabor.htm>.

Home - The National Agricultural Law Center. Web. <http://www.nationalaglawcenter.org/>.

National Association of State Departments of Agriculture Research Foundation. NASDA Home. Web. <http://www.nasda.org/>.

Erb, Kelly Phillips. *Kelly Phillips Erb - Taxgirl - Forbes*. Web. <http://www.taxgirl.com/>.

"Bankruptcy Basics." *United States Courts*. Web. <http://www.uscourts.gov/FederalCourts/Bankruptcy/BankruptcyBasics.aspx>.

United States Department of Agriculture, Farm Service Agency. Web. <www.fsa.usda.gov>

United States Department of Agriculture, Natural Resources Conservation Service. Web. <http://www.nrcs.usda.gov/>.

"YouthRules!" *United States Department of Labor*. Web. <http://www.youthrules.dol.gov>.

"U.S. Department of Labor - Wage and Hour Division (WHD) - Fact Sheet." *The U.S. Department of Labor Home Page*. Web. <http://www.dol.gov/whd/regs/compliance/whdfs12.htm>.

United States Patent and Trademark Office. Web. <http://www.uspto.gov/>.

Kunkel, Phillip L., Jeffrey A. Peterson, and Jessica A. Mitchell. "Bankruptcy: Chapter 12 Reorganization." *University of Minnesota Extension*. June 2009. Web. Dec. 2011. <http://www.extension.umn.edu/distribution/businessmanagement/df7301.html>.

Boswell, Chris. "Iowa DOT Transportation Rules." Web. <http://www.iowafarmbureau.com/article.aspx?articleID=38769>

Presentations

Meyer, Keith G, Steven C. Turner, Terry M. Anderson, Brooke Schuman, Patrick S. Turner. "UCC and Current Agricultural Issues." *The 2010

Annual Meeting of the American Agricultural Law Association. Presented 8 Oct. 2010.

McAfee Eldon L. "Iowa Environmental Regulations & Nuisance Case Update." *Presentation to Iowa Pork Congress.* Presented, 2011.

McAfee, Eldon L. "Agricultural Liens." *2011 Iowa State Bar Association, Commercial & Bankruptcy Law Seminar.* Presented 15 May 2011.

Thielen, Jim. "Complete Trust Course." *2011 PESI Continuing Education Course, Cedar Rapids, Iowa.* Presented 1 Dec. 2011

ABOUT THE AUTHOR

Pat Dillon is an Iowa farmer, who happens also to be an Iowa lawyer, frequently known to admit that he "became a lawyer to support his farming habit." Pat was born in Oelwein, Iowa, and grew up as part of a diversified family farm operation, graduating from Sumner Community Schools. Together with his brothers and his father, Pat operates a farm in northeast Iowa, with operations that include corn and soybean production, beef cattle, and timber management. Pat resides with his wife, Shelly, and three children, in a refurbished 1880's farm house near Sumner, and he practices law in the Sumner, Iowa, offices of Dillon Law, PC.

All protests aside, Pat Dillon also loves the law, and he takes genuine pleasure in catching problems early and in finding solutions to the legal issues, large and small, faced by his clients. Pat routinely represents clients in agricultural, real estate, estate planning, bankruptcy, and business issues.

Pat attended Iowa State University, earning a Bachelor of Science (with Distinction) in Agricultural Studies (Farm Operation), in 1997. Following four years of active duty service as a United States Army Transportation Officer, during which he Commanded the 513th Transportation Company and the 22d Transportation Detachment, Pat obtained his Juris Doctor (with High Honors) in 2003, from the Drake University Law School, in Des Moines, Iowa.

When you have a problem or have a question with ag law, Pat can be reached at 563 578 1850, through his website at www.50674law.com or email at book@50674law.com .

A

abstract of title, 133
accidents, 86–87
adverse possession, 139–141
advertisements, 26, 122.
    See also marketing
Ag Hazardous Occupation Orders, 96
agents, 38
agricultural liens, 65
2000 Agricultural Risk Protection Act, 115
agricultural workers, 93
air quality, 17
alcohol, 37, 83
animals. See also specific animals
    abandonment of, 8
    confinement of, 7
    control of, 7, 155–156
    death of, 18
    disposal of dead, 10, 153
    domesticated, 155
    endangered species, 11, 149, 155
    feeding operations and, 12–17
    importation of, 155
    neglect of, 156
    nuisance lawsuits and, 11–12
    physical examination of, 18
    protection of, 155
    sales of, 9
    treatment of, 18
    wild, 11, 155–156
APH (Approved Actual Production History Yield), 116
appeals, 17, 91, 129–131
Artificial Wetlands (AW), 2
Artisan's Liens, 65
assault, 83
assets, 28, 30, 60–63, 77, 120–121, 122–123, 128
ATVs, 49, 86
auction sales, 38–39
audits, 79
authority, persons without, 37
automatic stays, 31–32
Average Crop Revenue Election, 129

B

bailment law, 19
baiting, 11
bank stabilization, 2–3
bankruptcy
    Chapter 12 (farm reorganization), 30–31
    Chapter 7 (liquidation), 28–29, 71
    Chapter 13 (wage earner's plan), 29–30
    declaring, 76
    estates, 28
    notice of, 32
    trustees, 28
bees, 10, 154–155
beneficiaries, 54
benefits, 89, 90–91
"Beware of Dog" signs, 7
bodily injury, 85–86, 90–91
bonds, 79
bookkeepers, 94
borrowing and lending equipment, 86–87
breach of contract, 71
breeders, 24
bridge limits, 46
building restrictions, 147
burning, 151–152
businesses
    entity formalities and, 127–128
    formation of, 124–128
    industrial-style, 119–120
    planning of, 58, 122
    succession of, 54
    types of (See specific business types)

C

Camp and Pangborn, Tetzlaff v., 103
capital gains, 61, 120–121, 141, 142
Care of Stock Liens, 65
cash, 28
catastrophes, 40
cattle, 8, 39, 121. See also animals

C-Corporations (C-Corps), 58, 125
Certified Public Accountants (CPAs), 79
checks, 32–33, 76
chemicals, 150, 152–155
children, 57, 62, 94–96
Claim of Right, 140
claims, 28, 84, 90–91
Clean Air Act (CAA), 149, 151–152
Clean Water Act (CWA), 14, 149, 150–151
Code of Federal Regulations (CFR), 149
Color of Title, 140
commodities, 39, 40, 41, 69–73
Commodity Production Liens, 39, 65
communication, 97. See also notices, sending
Comprehensive Environmental Response Compensation and Liability Act (CERCLA), 149, 152
Concentrated Animal Feeding Operation (CAFO), 13–15
confinement operations, 16
conservation plans, 1
Conservation Reserve Enhancement Program (CREP), 3
Conservation Reserve Program (CRP), 3, 147
containment curbs, 51
contamination of ground water, 4
contracts. See also insurance; leases
    acceptance, 36
    breach of, 71
    capacity, 37
    cash-forward, 70
    Conservation Reserve Program (CRP) and, 3
    consideration of, 36
    credit sale, 76, 77, 79, 80
    custom feeding, 40–41
    deferred payment agreements, 70, 77
    employment, 37
    forming enforceable, 35–38
    futures, 70–71
    hedge-to-arrive (HTA), 71
    incapacity to form, 73
    informal, 128
    justification for failure to deliver, 71–72
    lease-to-own, 113
    minimum-price, 70
    mistakes, 37–38
    offers and, 35–36
    oral, 55–56
    price-later contracts, 70
    production, 39
    reversing, 71
    substantial performance of a, 38
copyrights, 25–26
corporations, 30–31, 47, 128. See also specific types
counter-cyclical payments, 129
creditors, 27, 28, 30, 31–32, 60
creek crossing work, 3
criminal laws, 11
criminal liability, 91
crops, 2, 11, 39, 72, 101–102, 155
Custom Cattle Feeding Liens, 65

D

death losses, 40
debtors, 27, 28, 29
debts, 29–33. See also bankruptcy
deeds, 133–134, 138
deer licenses, 11, 155
delivery deposits, 40
Department of Agriculture, 130
Department of Labor, 96
Department of Natural Resources (DNR), 11, 16, 49, 149
Department of Transportation (DOT), 43–46
deposits, 40, 105–106
de-tasseling, 95
dikes, 51
direct payments, 129
disasters, 17, 72
discharge, 14–15, 50
discipline, 97–98

ditch flushing systems, 14
documentation, 84–85
dogs, 7–8
dower/curtesy rights, 137–138
drainage issues, 1–5
drivers licenses, 45–46, 49
drunk persons, 37, 83
dumping, 153–154
dust, 152

E

earnest money, 36
easements, 4–5, 136–137, 147
elder generations, 57, 61–62
electrical sales rates, 146
emergency payment programs, 129
employees, 89–90, 93
employment contracts, 37
encumbrances, 65
endangered species, 11, 149, 155
Endangered Species Act (ESA), 149
environmental laws, 149–150
Environmental Protection Agency (EPA), 13, 15, 43, 149, 150–151, 152
Environmental Protection Commission, 17
Environmental Quality Incentives Program (EQIP), 3
equipment, farm, 86–87, 90, 112–113
equity, 28, 29, 31
estate planning
    balancing act of, 53–54, 53–55
    complexity of, 54
    definitions, 53–54
    gifts and, 63–64
    professional advice for, 55–56
    property ownership and, 60–63
    taxes and, 57
estimated production capabilities, 146
eviction, 107–111
excavating, 145–146
exit plans, 60
express easements, 5
express warranty, 9

F

failure to deliver, 71–72
Fair Labor Practices Act of 1938, 93
family farm corporations, 126
family members, 93
farm buildings, 2–3
farm cargo, 45
farm equipment, 86–87, 90, 112–113
farm operations, 2–3
farm reorganization, 30–31
Farm Service Agency (FSA), 10, 130–131, 154–155
Farmed Wetlands (FW), 2
Farmers Comprehensive Personal Liability (FCPL), 85–86
farmhouses, 119
farmowners insurance policies, 82
Federal Crop Insurance Act, 115
1994 Federal Crop Insurance Reform Act, 115
federal environmental laws, 149
Federal Environmental Protection Laws, 1–3, ix
federal gift tax law, 136
federal income taxes, 92
Federal Insecticide, Fungicide and Rodenticide Act (FIFRA), 149, 154–155
federal regulations. See specific regulations
feeding contracts, 40–41 @
feedlots, 41
fence laws, 143–144
fill and dredge activities, 151
finances, 54, 79–80
fines, 150
firearms, 11, 28, 155
Fish and Wildlife Division, 11, 155
flooding, 83
flushing systems, 14
flyovers, 15
forcible-entry-and-detainer action (FED), 109–111
forfeitures, 150
forms

1099, 92
AD-1026, 2
selecting, 126–127
UCC-1 statement, 102
W-2, 92
fuel, 49–52
fugitive dust, 152

G
game animals, 11, 155–156. *See also* animals
game laws, 11, 155
genetically modified organisms (GMOs), 24
gifts, 63–64, 136
goals, 97
grain carts, 43
grain dealer licensing, 78–80
grain elevators, 151
Grain Indemnity Fund. *See* Iowa Grain Indemnity Fund
grains, 48, 69–70, 76, 151
ground, disturbing the, 3

H
habitats, 11, 155
hail, 116
harvest prices, 116
Harvester's Liens, 65
hay, 3
hazardous chemicals, 152–155
hazardous work, 96
hedging, 71
heirs, 54–60, 99
highly erodible land (HEL), 1, 3
hobby farms, 121–124
horses, 86, 121
hourly rates, 93
household goods, 28
hunting, 11

I
implement of husbandry, 43

implied easements, 5
incinerators, 151
income, 31, 57
income taxes, 55, 92, 120–121, 136
indemnity, 75–76, 103
independent contractors, 89–90, 92
industrial-style business, 119–120
injuries, bodily, 85–86, 90–91
inspections, 48, 80
insurance
    coverage types, 83–84
    deductibles, 82
    documentation and, 84–85
    exclusions, 83
    farmowners insurance policies, 82
    inventory and, 84–85
    liability, 81–82, 85–87
    losses, 84–85
    motor vehicle insurance, 82
    Multi-Peril Crop Insurance (MPCI), 115–117
    photographs used for, 84–85
    policies, 82
    premiums, 82
    property damage or losses and, 72–73, 75–76, 83–84, 84–85
    riders, 83
    self-, 91
    workman's compensation, 90–91
intellectual property (IP), 21
interest, 61, 134–135
interests, competing, 57
inventions, 21, 22–25
inventory, 84
Iowa Code Section 203.1(10), 78
Iowa Department of Agriculture and Land Stewardship (IDALS), 75–76, 78–79
Iowa Environmental Protection Laws, 4–5
Iowa Grain Indemnity Fund, 75, 76, 77
Iowa Property Laws and Drainage Changes, 4–5
Iowa's Estate Recovery Team, 62
IRS regulations
    1099 reporting rules, 92

20/20 test, 113
eligibility for depreciation, 47
family members and, 64
feed bills and, 41
hobby farms and, 121–124
"like kind" exchanges, 142

J
jail time, 150
joint tenancy with rights of survivorship (JTWRS), 61, 135

L
labor, 57
labor laws, 89–98
lagoons, 151
landlord's checklist, 111–112
landlord's lien, 102
Landlord's liens, 65
last will and testament, 53
laws, 89–98, 143–144, 149–150
leadership, 97–98
leases. *See also* liens
    breaches, 107–111
    eviction and, 107–111
    farm acreage, 99–104
    farm equipment and, 112–113
    habitability and, 106
    pricing, 113
    renting and, 104–113
    security deposits and, 105–106
    tenant obligations and, 107–108
    termination of, 101, 107–108
    terms, 100–101
    to-own, 112–113
    wind-energy, 147
legally insane persons, 37
lending and borrowing equipment, 86–87
letter of credit, 79
liability, 59, 81–82, 85–87, 91, 128
licensed dealers, 77
licenses
    application of pesticides and, 154–155
    deer, 11, 155
    grain dealers and, 78–80
    revoking of, 76
liens, 39, 65–67, 102, 136. *See also* leases
life estates, 62–63, 135
"like kind" exchanges, 142
Limited Liability Companies (LLCs), 47, 58, 59, 126, 128
limited partnerships, 58, 59, 125
liquidation bankruptcy, 28–29, 71
livestock, 9, 39, 121. *See also* animals
loan deficiency payments, 129
loans, 27–32
losses, 84–85

M
malpractice cases, 17–19
management burdens, 56
manure, 40, 150
Manure Management Plan (MMP), 15–16
marketing, 26, 40, 69, 122
marriage and property rights, 137–138
master matrix, 17
Material Data Safety Sheet, 155
Mechanic's Liens, 65
Medicaid liens, 63, 136
medical certification cards, 46–47
medical coverage, 90–91
Migratory Bird Treaty Act (MBTA), 149
minimum wage, 93–94
minors, 37, 45, 94–96. *See also* children
money, 58
motor vehicles, 11, 82, 155–156
mowing, 3
Multi-Peril Crop Insurance (MPCI), 115–117

N
National Pollutant Discharge Elimination System (NPDES), 14–15, 150

natural disasters, 72
Natural Resources Conservation Service (NRCS), 1–3, 130
negligence, 19, 40, 72, 81, 85
net worth, 79
nitrogen, 4
notices, sending, 33, 107, 110, 111, 112, 130–131
noxious weeds, 156
nuisance lawsuits, 11–12

O
Occupational Safety and Health Act (OSHA), 94
oil, 153–154
One Call, 145
open field burning, 151
oral contracts, 55–56, 99
organization, 97–98
overtime pay, 93–94
ownership rights, 21, 22–25

P
Packers and Stockyard Act, 9
partnerships, 30–31, 47, 58–59, 125
patents, 21, 22–25, 26
payments, 65–66, 77, 129
paystubs, 92
penalties, 149–150
permits
  National Pollutant Discharge Elimination System (NPDES), 14–15
  Number 40, 2
  Section 404, 2–3
  water use, 4
pesticides, 4, 10, 149, 150, 152, 154–155
pets. *See* animals; specific pets
phosphorus index, 16
photographs, 84, 111
pitfalls, 120
pits, 51
plagiarism, 25
Plant Variety Protection Act, 24

police, 110–111
pollution, 13–15, 150
possession, adverse, 139–141
power of attorney, 54
Power Purchase Agreement, 146
power transfer, 62–63
prescriptive easements, 5
pricing protections, 70
Prior Converted (PC), 2
probate, 61, 62, 63
producers, 24–25, 78
production costs, 69
production guarantee, 116–117
profits, 123
property
  abandonment of, 32
  damages, 8, 83–84
  exempt, 28
  fence laws and, 143–144
  insurance and, 83–85
  joint ownership of, 134–135
  marriage rights and, 137–138
  ownership of, 60–63, 134–135
  purchasing, 138–139
  rights, 11–12
  trespassers and, 143
protections pricing, 70
puffing, 9, 39
purchases, 80, 85, 138–139

Q
quicklime, 10
Quitclaim Deeds, 133–134

R
rabies vaccinations, 7, 8
range production of livestock, 93
raw agricultural products
  transportation, 47–48
real estate. *See* leases
record-keeping, 80, 122, 154–155
registration, false, 47
regulations
  agriculture and, 149–156

Code of Federal Regulations (CFR), 149
Department of Transportation (DOT) and, 43–46
Federal Environmental Protection Laws and, 1
IRS and, 41, 47, 64, 92, 113, 121–124, 142
soils and, 1
water and, 3–4
related party rule, 64
Renewable Energy Credits (REC), 146–147
rental agreements, 104–113
replanting seeds, 24
res ipsa loquitur, 18
researchers, 24
Resource and Conservation Recovery Act (RCRA), 149, 153
restrictions, building, 147
Revenue Protection Plans, 117
Risk Management Agency (RMA), 115
risk managing, 71
road work, 3
runoff, 150

S
safety chains, 44
sales, 76, 77–78
salvage tags, 11, 156
scale house tickets, 70
S-Corporations (S-Corps), 58, 59, 126
secured creditors, 27–28
security deposits, 105–106
security interest, 77
seeds, 24–25
self-insured, 91
separation distances, 13
Service Animal Liens, 65
servicemarks, 25
settlement sheets, 80
sham corporations, 128
shareholders, 31, 58, 125, 126, 147
signs, 7, 10

social security taxes, 92
sodbusters, 1, 2
soil, 1, 3. *See also* ground, disturbing the; wetlands
Soil Commission, 3
sole proprietorships, 47, 58, 79, 124
spills, 150
spouses, 60–63, 137–138
state employment insurance taxes, 92
state income taxes, 92
state laws, 149
statute of limitations, 139
stock, 31
stockyards, 9
substantial performance, 38
succession planning, 56–57, 59
suing, 77, 91
Superfund Act, 152
swampbusters, 1

T
taxes
    basis, 141–142
    benefits, 128
    brackets, 121
    capital gains, 61, 120–121, 141, 142
    C-Corporations and, 58
    consequences and, 41, 57, 120
    considerations for, 120–121
    deductions, 84, 121
    estate, 57
    federal, 92, 120–121
    gifts and, 63–64, 136
    identification number used for, 89
    income, 55, 92, 120–121, 136
    life estates and, 63
    "like kind" exchanges and, 142
    Limited Liability Companies (LLCs) and, 59
    noxious weeds and, 156
    partnerships and, 58–59
    planning for, 54, 70, 77, 141–143
    S-Corporations and, 58
    social security, 92

state, 92, 120–121
    withholding, 92
telephone numbers, 145
tenancy in common (TIC), 61, 135
tenants, 107–108
Tetzlaff v. Camp and Pangborn, 103
theft charges, 33
threats, 33
tile drain easements, 4
tires, 153–154
titles, 9, 101–102, 133, 139
tools, 28
towing, 44
tractors, 43. *See also* vehicles
trademarks, 25
transfer of power, 62–63
transportation, 43–51. *See also* vehicles
trespassing, 8, 143
trucks, 47–48. *See also* vehicles
trusts, 53–54

U
underground network activities, 145
Underground Storage Tanks (USTs), 154
unemployment, 92
United States Department of Agriculture (USDA), 24, 76
United States Patent and Trademark Office (USPTO), 21, 25
unsecured creditors, 28
utility line back fill, 2

V
vaccinations, 8

vehicles, 28, 43–49, 86, 155–156. *See also* equipment; specific vehicles
veterinarians, 17–19, 65
Veterinarian's Liens, 65
violations, 129
visitors, 143–144

W
wage earner's plan, 29–30
warehouses, 69–70, 75–76
warranties, 9
Warranty Deeds, 133–134
waste, 153–154
water, 1–2, 14–15, 150–151
weeds, 156
wells, 4
Wetland Reserve Program (WEP), 3
wetlands, 2–3, 151
wild animals, 11, 155–156. *See also* animals
wills, 53
wind energy, 146–147
Workman's Compensation Commission, 90–91
Writ of Removal, 111

Y
100-year floodplan, 13
Yield Protection Plans, 117

Z
zoning ordinances, 144–145

Made in the USA
Lexington, KY
06 August 2012